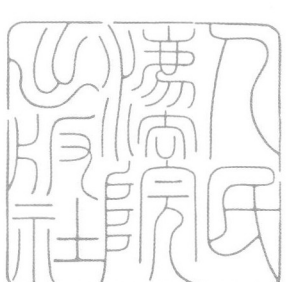

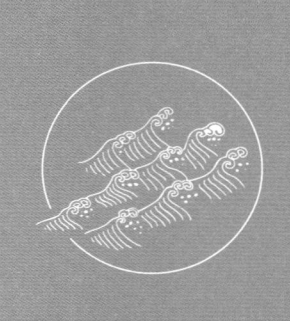

前 言
Foreword

Guanzi said, "The law is the formula of the world and the gauge of all things." [i]

Shang Yang said, "Laws and regulations are the foundation of governance." [ii]

Han Fei said, "The law does not favor the nobility, just as the plumb line does not yield to the crooked wood." [iii]

...

General Secretary Xi Jinping noted, "The Chinese legal system has a long history, and its fine traditional legal culture contains rich thinking about the rule of law and profound political wisdom, making it a treasure of Chinese culture." [iv]

管子曰:"法者,天下之程式也,万事之仪表也。"①

商鞅云:"法令者,民之命也,为治之本也。"②

韩非言:"法不阿贵,绳不挠曲。"③

……

习近平总书记指出:"中华法系源远流长,中华优秀传统法律文化蕴含丰富法治思想和深邃政治智慧,是中华文化的瑰宝。"④

---

[i] Excerpted from *Guanzi*. It means that law serves as the standard for governing the realm and as the model for all matters.

[ii] Excerpted from *The Book of Lord Shang*. It means that laws and regulations are the basis for people to survive and the foundation of governance.

[iii] Excerpted from *Han Feizi*. It means that the law does not favor the nobility, just as the plumb line does not yield to the crooked wood.

[iv] Excerpted from the speech by General Secretary Xi Jinping at the 10th group study session of the Political Bureau of the Communist Party of China Central Committee (November 27, 2023), http://english.www.gov.cn/news/202311/28/content_WS65658e5dc6d0868f4e8e1b37.html.

① 出自《管子·明法解》,意思是:法律是治理天下的准则,是一切事物的规范标准。

② 出自《商君书·定分》,意思是:法令是百姓生存的根本,是治理国家的基础。

③ 出自《韩非子·有度》,意思是:法律不偏袒权贵,如同木工的墨线不向弯曲的地方倾斜。

④ 习近平总书记在中共中央政治局第十次集体学习时的讲话(2023年11月27日),载《人民日报》2023年11月29日,第1版。

Magnificent is the Chinese civilization, vast is this ancient land, where sages' eternal quest for the essence of law flows unbroken. In the ancient times when "The Adjudication of Gao Yao", our ancestors had developed an early form of law. Duke Zhou's "ritual and music making" laid the foundation for the culture of ritual and law. During the Spring and Autumn Period and the Warring States Period, Legalist thought flourished, and written laws were disseminated to the masses. Since the Qin and Han dynasties, the written legal system has been fully established, culminating in a fully developed legal framework. In the prosperous Tang Dynasty, the legal culture transcended national borders and radiated to other Asian countries.

With thousands of years of history, in the dimension of "law", how many shining names and allusions are there in history that are worth looking up to and admiring? This time, we use original accounts as a carrier, attempting to focus on those visionary minds, wise and profound insights, rich and great ideas, and selfless righteousness in the long river of Chinese legal culture. Throughout history, many great minds in law have left a lasting mark. Some were thinkers whose insights stirred the minds of generations. Some were politicians advancing legal practice with resolve. Some were codifiers who crafted the legal systems with masterful skills. Others were jurists who interpreted the

巍巍中华，泱泱古国，先贤们对"法"的叩问和求索，生生不息。溯至上古"皋陶决狱"，法律雏形已现端倪；周公"制礼作乐"，奠定中华礼法文化之基；春秋战国，不同法律思想绽放异彩，法律条文"布之于众"；秦汉以降，成文法体系广泛确立，法制规范规模已成；及至盛唐，法制文明超越国界，辐射亚洲诸国。

华夏历史数千载，长河浩瀚；法脉传承贯今古，熠熠生辉。在"法律"这一维度上，深邃的思想绵延不绝，崇高的精神灿若星辰，无私的正气经久不衰。众多法律人物在历史深处恒久闪烁，他们或为思想家，以睿智的见地启发人心；或是为政者，以坚定的意志推动法律实践；或为法典编修人，以精湛的技艺构筑法律体系；或为法学家，以深刻的哲思诠释法律真谛。这些杰出的法律人物和法治故事，不仅承载了法律文化民族品格，也为今天提供了丰富的滋养和启迪。

essence of law through profound reflection. These remarkable figures and the legal tales associated with them embody the moral character of Chinese legal culture and continue to nourish us today.

The Origin of Law: An Illustrated Reader of Fine Traditional Chinese Legal Culture (Chinese-English) brings this legacy to life with Gongbi (meticulous-style) paintings, portraying 15 legendary legal figures and 15 stories that echo across centuries. After a year of design conception, material selection, meticulous painting, and copywriting, we focused on studying portraits of people, setting up visual scenes, and contemplating the costumes and artifacts of their respective dynasties in painting and depiction. We strive to be faithful to historical materials and strive for accuracy and precision in copywriting. Drawing on the established theories and views in legal historiography, this book seeks to extract the core spirit of Chinese legal civilization, preserve its cultural lineage, and distill the essence of its timeless values.

This book has been made possible with the guidance of China Institute of Legal History, led by President Zhang Sheng, and the generous support of many others. In particular, Professor Luo Guannan, Associate Professor Li Dejia, and Lecturer Li Chi have helped proofread the manuscript at different stages. We would like to express our gratitude to them all.

《法本——中华优秀传统法律文化图说（中英文版）》以古雅的原创工笔绘画，呈现中国历史上15位名贯古今的法律人物，讲述15则蕴意宏远的法治故事。经过一年时间设计构思、绘画创作、文案推敲，我们着力考据人物肖像、斟酌服饰器物；在素材选择上忠实史料，力求简明精当；在内容阐述上参读法史学权威观点，力图提炼中华法治文明精神标识，赓续法律文化精神血脉，萃取优秀传统法律文化价值精髓。

《法本——中华优秀传统法律文化图说（中英文版）》创作过程中，得中国法律史学会指导，张生会长、罗冠男教授、李德嘉副教授、李驰讲师审核，以及相关人士出谋划策、贡献智识。所有关怀和帮助恕不另述，同此致谢！

习近平总书记指出："'求木之长者，必固其根本；欲流之远者，必浚其泉源。'中华优秀传统文化是中华民族的精神命脉，是涵养社会主义核心价值观的重要源泉，也是我

As General Secretary Xi Jinping remarked, "'If you want a tree to grow tall, help it grow strong roots; if you want a river to flow far, help its source flow smoothly.' The best of China's traditional culture is the lifeblood of the Chinese nation. It provides fertile soil for the core socialist values and the foundation for the nation to gain a firm foothold in global cultural interaction."[i]

The enduring Chinese civilization has cultivated a unique legal system, rich in cultural depth and radiant in its legal achievements. *The Origin of Law: An Illustrated Reader of Fine Traditional Chinese Legal Culture (Chinese-English)* presents selected legal figures and stories—some familiar, others perhaps new to you—that contribute to Chinese legal heritage. It is hoped that this book will bolster steadfast confidence in the rule of law and enable us to draw inspiration from China's outstanding traditional legal culture.

们在世界文化激荡中站稳脚跟的坚实根基。"①

绵延不断的中华文明孕育了世界上独树一帜的中华法系，积淀了深厚的文化，创造了灿烂的中华法治文明。《法本——中华优秀传统法律文化图说（中英文版）》精选的法律人物和故事，也许为你熟知，或许是你未识，但在法律文化赓续上，相信这本画册有助于我们坚定法治自信，不断从灿烂的中华优秀传统法律文化中汲取丰厚的历史滋养。

---

i Excerpted from the speech by Xi Jinping at the Forum on Literature and Art (October 15. 2014), http://en.qstheory.cn/2025-01/13/c_1063923.htm.

① 习近平在文艺工作座谈会上的讲话（2014年10月15日），载新华网，http://www.xinhuanet.com/politics/2015-10/14/c_1116825558.htm。

目 录
Contents

3	皋陶 Gao Yao	27	楚庄王茅门之法 King Zhuang of Chu's Law of the Mao Gate
7	皋陶决狱 The Adjudication of Gao Yao	29	子产铸刑书 Zichan's Casting of Code of Laws
10	周公制礼作乐 Duke of Zhou: Architect of the Ritual and Music System	31	李悝 Li Kui
13	管仲 Guan Zhong	35	李离过杀伏剑 Li Li's Suicide After Ordering an Unjust Execution
19	邓析 Deng Xi	37	商鞅 Shang Yang
24	邓析"两可说" Deng Xi's "Theory of Dual Possibilities"	41	商鞅徙木立信 Shang Yang: Establishing Credibility by Rewarding People for Moving a Log

43	荀况 Xun Kuang	73	长孙无忌 Zhangsun Wuji
48	百人逐兔 A Hundred People Chasing a Rabbit	77	唐太宗览图禁杖 Emperor Taizong of Tang Banned Caning After Reviewing the Acupuncture Diagram
51	韩非 Han Fei	79	唐太宗与"五复奏" Emperor Taizong of Tang and the "Five-Review System"
55	张释之 Zhang Shizhi	81	包拯 Bao Zheng
59	张释之不阿上意 Zhang Shizhi: Not Yielding to Imperial Will	85	宋慈 Song Ci
61	汉文帝废肉刑 The Abolition of Corporal Punishment by Emperor Wen of Han	89	王阳明爱民如子 Wang Yangming: Governing with Compassion
63	张汤审鼠 Zhang Tang's Trial of the Mouse	91	黄宗羲 Huang Zongxi
65	杜预 Du Yu	95	沈家本 Shen Jiaben
69	刘颂 Liu Song	100	六尺巷：一诗化干戈 The Six-foot Alley: A Poem Turns Conflict into Harmony

Contributions   Legend has it that Gao Yao composed the *Code of Penalty* (*Yu Dian*), the earliest legal code in Chinese history. He had it inscribed on tree bark and submitted it to Yu, who praised its principles and ordered its implementation. Gao Yao's approach to law enforcement was characterized by strictness, impartiality, and fairness: leniency for accidental offenses, strict penalties for intentional or repeat crimes, and light sentences for cases with any doubts. He believed that the ultimate purpose of punishment was to eliminate the need for it, fostering people's "awareness of the Five Penalties" to maintain social order. In governance, Gao Yao championed the benevolent rule, stressing that only individuals of integrity and ability, diligence, and incorruptibility could secure a peaceful and harmonious society. He was also credited with advancing agricultural productivity by inventing Leisi—a kind of tilling tool. It was Gao Yao's full support that enabled the prosperity in the era of Yao, Shun, and Yu, paving the way for the "Early State Stage."

Legacy   As a distinguished statesman, philosopher, jurist, and educator of ancient China, Gao Yao was entrusted with the administration of justice and moral guidance. He upheld the idea of "developing awareness of legal punishments to facilitate moral guidance, thereby civilizing the people."

成就

传说我国第一部法典《狱典》由皋陶制定，他把《狱典》刻在树皮上，呈送禹看后，禹颇为赞许，命皋陶实施。皋陶执法严昭、公允，对过失犯罪者予以宽待，对故意犯罪或累犯不改者从严处罚，对罪疑者从轻发落；主张施刑是为了无刑，使民众"明于五刑"，才能行止有序。皋陶在政治上主张施行德政，认为举用德才兼备、勤政廉洁之人方能民安世治。相传皋陶还发明了耒耜（lěi sì，似犁的农具），为发展农业生产作出了贡献。皋陶的鼎力辅佐使尧舜禹时代出现了繁荣盛世，迈进"早期国家阶段"。

评价

皋陶是上古时期著名的政治家、思想家、法学家、教育家，执掌司法和教化工作，主张"明刑弼教，以化万民"，不仅"流布

Life Story

Gao Yao, bearing the surname Ying, was born in Qufu (or Gaoyao Village, Hongtong County, Shanxi Province in alternative records). During the reigns of Yao, Shun, and Yu, he served as Shishi [i] (or Daliguan, Minister of Justice), overseeing judicial and penal affairs. His maxim, "Use the Five Penalties to assist the Five Moral Principles," [ii] underscored the philosophy of integrating legal enforcement with moral guidance, asserting that punishment should serve as a supplement to moral instruction. After Yu ascended to the throne, tensions arose among the states in the Jianghuai region. Gao Yao thus toured the region several times to extol Yu's tireless efforts to alleviate flooding and his selfless devotion to the people. His endeavors ultimately led the region to become awed by the feat of Yu and be grateful for his benevolent deeds, winning their allegiance. Gao Yao remained a close advisor during Yu's reign. As recorded in *Records of the Grand Historian*, Yu intended to abdicate the throne in favor of Gao Yao. However, Gao Yao passed away before Yu, reportedly at the age of 106. He was buried in Lu—now Lu'an, Anhui Province. For ancestral worship, Yu enfeoffed the land of Lu to the descendants of Gao Yao, who was hence called the "Forefather of Lu'an State."

---

i As noted in the "Canon of Shun" in *Shang Shu*, "Gao Yao, it is your duty, as the Shi, to use the Five Penalties to deal with their offenses." Here, "Shi" refers to "Shishi (Minister of Justice)", a key official responsible for legal and penal matters during the reigns of Shun and Yu.

ii This maxim implies the prudent application of the Five Penalties to reinforce the Five Cardinal Relationships, embodying the ancient governance philosophy of "using punishment to assist virtue."

生 平

皋陶，姓嬴，生于曲阜（一说生于山西洪洞县皋陶村）。在尧、舜、禹时期担任士师①（后世文献中亦称"大理官"），负责执掌司法和刑罚事务。其"明于五刑，以弼五教"②，主张将刑罚作为辅助手段，强调法治与德治相结合的重要性。禹继位后，江淮各部落对禹有不满情绪，皋陶多次巡视江淮，宣说大禹不畏艰险、公而忘私、一心为民排除水患的功绩，终使江淮地区畏威怀德，一致拥戴大禹。皋陶在禹时期继续辅佐治理国家事务，《史记》记载禹曾有意禅让帝位给皋陶，但皋陶先于禹去世，相传活到 106 岁。逝世后被安葬于六，即今安徽六安。为便于祭祀，禹将六分封给皋陶后裔，皋陶因此也被称为"六安国始祖"。

---

① 见于《尚书·舜典》："皋陶，汝作士，五刑有服。"这里的"士"即"士师"，舜禹时代的核心官员之一，主管法律和刑狱。

② 意为审慎运用五刑，以辅助五伦教化，体现上古"刑以辅德"的治理理念。

His efforts to cultivate social morals extended beyond "disseminating the Five Moral Principles"[i] to civilize and guide the people, and included administering by making laws and setting up prisons. Gao Yao is revered as the "Founder of Chinese Judicature"; together with Yao, Shun, and Yu, Gao Yao is honored as one of the "Four Sages of Ancient Times." As a treasure of traditional Chinese legal culture, his thought emphasized the integration of law and morality, and the combination between rule of law and rule of virtue, and still holds much significance for today's construction of the rule of law.

五教"[①]教化、引导民众，同时通过制法作狱手段治理民众，以此达到纯良社会风气的目的。皋陶被尊为"中国司法鼻祖"，与尧、舜、禹被后世并称为"上古四圣"，其思想作为中国传统法律文化的代表，强调法律与道德相统一、法治与德治相结合，对今天的法治建设仍具有重要意义。

---

[i] It refers to the dissemination of the Five Cardinal Relationships, which are commonly interpreted as "father-son, ruler-subject, husband-wife, elder brother-younger brother, and friend-friend relationships" as recorded in *Mencius*.

[①] 意为广泛推行五种伦理教化。"五教"的主流解释为《孟子·滕文公上》所载"父子、君臣、夫妇、长幼、朋友"之教。

皋陶决狱

相传，上古时期的司法长官、被誉为我国"司法鼻祖"的皋陶在决讼听狱①时，有一只名为獬豸（xiè zhì）的神兽伴其左右。獬豸形似麒麟，长有一角，能辨是非曲直，识善恶忠奸，触邪妄不正。皋陶遇疑难未决之案，其罪疑者，令獬豸触之，有罪则触，无罪则不触。这个传说体现了上古时"神明裁判"的神秘色彩。獬豸决讼实则赞美皋陶公正智慧、执法无私，獬豸也由此成为中国传统法律文化中公平正义的象征。

The Adjudication of Gao Yao

As legend has it, Gao Yao, the ancient judicial officer hailed as the "founder of Chinese judicature," had a mythical creature named Xiezhi by his side when adjudicating cases.[i] This beast resembling a Chinese unicorn was believed to have the extraordinary ability to discern good from bad and identify virtue and loyalty, revealing any form of evil and injustice. Encountering difficult or undecided cases, Gao Yao would instruct Xiezhi to approach the accused. Xiezhi would strike who was guilty with its horn, and remain still if the suspect was innocent. This story reflects the mystical nature of "divine judgment" in ancient times. Ultimately, the tale of Xiezhi helping with adjudication was intended to praise Gao Yao's integrity, wisdom, and impartiality in law enforcement, and Xiezhi has become a symbol of fairness and justice in traditional Chinese legal culture.

---

① "决讼"指审理民事纠纷，"听狱"指审判刑事案件。

i *Juesong*（决讼）refers to adjudicating civil disputes, while *tingyu*（听狱）pertains to the trial of criminal cases.

周公制礼作乐

西周礼乐制度相传为周公所制。周公是西周初期重要的政治家和文化领袖，姓姬，名旦，周文王之子、武王之弟，曾助武王灭商。武王死后摄政，推行了一系列政治文化改革，其中包括制礼作乐。周公所制之礼乃西周政治准则、道德规范、典章制度的总称，所制之乐则为贵族举办礼仪活动之舞乐，其规模和形式与不同社会等级相对应。周公制礼作乐将伦理道德与法律规范融为一体，被视为中华礼法文化的源头，体现了中华法治文明以礼入法、礼法并用的理念。

Duke of Zhou: Architect of the Ritual and Music System

The ritual and music system of the Western Zhou Dynasty is said to have been established by the Duke of Zhou, a pivotal statesman and cultural leader at the dawn of that dynasty. Named Ji Dan, Duke of Zhou was a son of King Wen of Zhou, and the younger brother of King Wu of Zhou. He once assisted King Wu in overthrowing the Shang Dynasty. As part of his sweeping political and cultural reforms, he introduced the ritual and music system. The rituals designed by the Duke of Zhou encompassed the overarching political, moral, and institutional standards of the Western Zhou Dynasty, while the music referred to the dance and musical performances in aristocratic ceremonial occasions, with scales and forms tailored to different social strata. Integrating ethics with legal norms, the Duke of Zhou's ritual and music system is regarded as the origin of China's culture of law and rite, embodying the governance philosophy of "embedding rite into legal frameworks to create a unified system of governance upholding both rite and law."

Life Story

Guan Zhong, also known as Yiwu (courtesy name Zhong), was a native of Yingshang (now Yingshang, Anhui Province). In his early years, he engaged in commerce. Later, recommended by Bao Shuya, he became a minister of Duke Huan of Qi. During his tenure, he implemented a series of reforms, promoting capable individuals and strengthening the state's wealth and military power. Domestically, he developed industry, commerce, fishing, salt production, and iron smelting. Externally, he pursued the strategy of "honoring the king and expelling the barbarians," supporting the authority of the Zhou king while forming alliances with various feudal lords. He assisted Duke Huan of Qi in "uniting the feudal lords nine times and bringing order to the entire country," launching campaigns against the Shanrong in the north and the State of Chu in the south, ultimately establishing Duke Huan as the first hegemon of the Spring and Autumn Period. After his death, he was buried at Mountain Niushan in Linzi.

Contributions

While assisting Duke Huan of Qi, Guan Zhong implemented a series of major reforms. In administration, he introduced the "Three Capital Zones and Five Outer Districts" [i] system to

---

[i] "Three Capital Zones": It indicates the division of the national capital into three administrative regions, governed separately by the Duke of Qi and the noble families of Gao and Guo.

"Five Outer Districts": It refers to the establishment of a five-tiered administrative system in rural areas, comprising levels of Shu (district), Xian (commandery), Xiang (township), Zu (battalion), and Yi (village), each with designated officers for hierarchical management. Through this reform, Guan Zhong created a "militia-farmer integration" system, consolidating central authority.

生 平

管仲，名夷吾，字仲，颍上（今安徽颍上）人。早年经商，后经鲍叔牙举荐，任齐桓公卿相，执政期间采取一系列改革措施，举贤任能、富国强兵，对内发展工商、渔盐、冶铁等，对外推行"尊王攘夷"策略，拥护周天子，同时与各诸侯国会盟，辅佐齐桓公"九合诸侯，一匡天下"，北击山戎、南伐楚国，成为春秋第一霸主。晚年病逝后葬于临淄牛山。

成 就

管仲在辅佐齐桓公期间进行了一系列重大改革：在行政管理上首创"三国五鄙"①制度，对不同行政区划分级管理，与后世郡县制有相通之处。在人才选

---

① "三国"：将国都（城邑）划分为三个行政区域，由齐君与两大贵族家族高氏、国氏分治。"五鄙"：在郊野（农村）建立"属→县→乡→卒→邑"五级管理体系，设官分级统辖。管仲通过此改革实现了兵农合一的目的，强化了中央集权。

establish hierarchical governance over different administrative regions. The system was later echoed in the prefecture-county system. When selecting officials, he "honored the virtuous and nurtured talent," breaking aristocracy's monopoly and stressing merit-based appointment. In terms of economy, he initiated land reform, imposing graded tax based on land quality, and allowing household-based land contract. He even pioneered the state monopoly on salt and iron and implemented a price-stabilization mechanism to regulate market prices. In military affairs, he created a "militia-farmer" system, and through the "expelling the barbarians" strategy, he helped secure Qi's dominance as a hegemonic state.

Guan Zhong was the earliest advocate for the rule of law, believing that "the law is the formula of the world and the gauge of all things." He argued that "everyone, regardless of status, should abide by the law," which embodied the principle of equality before the law. Guan Zhong emphasized that the sovereign must not only enact laws but also adhere to them. "If the ruler does not follow the law, the people will not comply," rendering the laws ineffective. In enforcement, he stressed that "decrees preceding all actions," embedding the rule of law into every administration facet. His legislative philosophy emphasized that "laws and decrees must align with the will of the people," seeking to harmonize laws, heavenly principles, and public sentiment. At the same time, Guan Zhong valued the role of moral education, stating that "propriety, righteousness, integrity, and a sense of shame are the four pillars of the state," considering

拔上"尊贤育才"，打破贵族垄断，重视选贤任能。在经济上实施土地改革，按土地等级征税，允许农民家庭承包土地，首创盐铁国家专营，设立"平准法"调控物价。在军事上建立"兵民合一"制度，通过"攘夷"方略确立齐国霸主地位。

管仲最早提出"以法治国"理念，认为"法者，天下之程式，万事之仪表"，主张"君臣上下贵贱皆从法"，体现了法律面前人人平等的思想，认为君主不仅立法而且必须依法行事，否则"上不行则民不从"，法必然无法施行。在法令的执行上强调"凡将举事，令必先出"，把以法治国贯彻到施政的各个方面。在立法上主张"法令要顺应民心"，重视法理情的统一。同时管仲也看重道德教化的作用，认为"礼义廉耻，国之四维"，将其视为国家治理的重要因素。特别强调民富之后要继之以教化，所谓"仓廪实而知礼节，衣食足而知荣辱"。管仲的法治理念被梁

them essential to national governance. He particularly emphasized that "once the people are rich, they must be educated," as reflected in his famous saying: "When granaries are full, the people understand propriety; when food and clothing are sufficient, they understand honor and shame." Guan Zhong's legal philosophy is regarded by Liang Qichao as the origin of China's rule-of-law thought. Liang praised him as "the first to articulate the doctrine of rule of law, establishing a unique school of thought." [i]

Legacy

Guan Zhong was a representative figure of the Legalist School during the Spring and Autumn Period, renowned as an ancient statesman, economist, and military strategist. For his role in assisting Duke Huan of Qi in achieving hegemony, he is celebrated as "the greatest minister of all time." Confucius once praised his efforts in preserving the civilization of Zhou rituals through the "equal emphasis on ritual and law." Sima Qian described him as "issuing decrees like the flow of a river's source, ensuring they align with the will of the people," succinctly capturing his wisdom in governance, particularly his practice of "observing customs to establish laws." Guan Zhong is regarded by later generations as a

启超认为是我国法治思想源头，称赞其"最初发明法治主义以成一家之言"。①

评 价

管仲是春秋时期法家代表人物，古代著名的政治家、经济学家、军事家，因辅佐齐桓公成就霸业被称为"千古一相"。孔子赞扬其通过"礼法并举"存续周礼文明；司马迁称其"下令如流水之原，令顺民心"，精准概括了他在国家治理中"观俗立法"的智慧。管仲被后世认为是"以法治国"理念的先驱，《管子》记载了他"以法治国，则举措而已"的思想，对后世的

---

[i] Liang Qichao. *The History of Political Thought in the Pre-Qin Era*, Zhonghua Book Company, 2016.

① 梁启超《先秦政治思想史》，中华书局2016年版。

pioneer of the concept of "governing the state by law." *The Guanzi* records his philosophy that "to govern the state by law is to act with decisive measures," which profoundly influenced later generations' governance theories and political practices.

The phrase "define rights and resolve disputes" originates from "Seven Ministers and Seven Rulers" in *Guanzi*: "Law is established to promote merit and deter violence. Rules are designed to define rights and resolve disputes. Decrees are issued to inform the people of administrative matters." [i]

Zhang Jun, President and Chief Justice of the Supreme People's Court of People's Republic of China, has repeatedly emphasized that "defining rights and obligations" is the basic requirement for a fair judiciary and the premise of "resolving disputes" by means of law to clarify right and wrong, good and evil, and determine the ownership of rights. [ii] He urged people's courts at all levels to thoroughly implement Xi Jinping Thought on the Rule of Law, and effectively ensure judicial fairness and settle social disputes.

治国理念和政治实践产生了深远影响。

"定分止争"典出《管子·七臣七主》："法者，所以兴功惧暴也；律者，所以定分止争也；令者，所以令人知事也。"①

最高人民法院院长张军多次强调，"定分"是以法律手段明是非善恶、定权利归属，是公正司法的基本要求，是"止争"的前提，②要求全国各级人民法院深入贯彻习近平法治思想，切实做到公正司法、定分止争。

---

[i] Meaning of this quote: Law functions to promote merit and deter violence; rules are designed to define ownerships and resolve disputes; decrees are issued to guide the people so they can understand various affairs.

[ii] "The Fengqiao Model for Promoting Community-level Governance in the New Era: Defining Rights with Emphasis on Resolving Disputes," posted on the website of the Supreme People's Court of the People's Republic of China, November 14, 2024. https://www.court.gov.cn/zixun/xiangqing/447501.html.

① 意思是：法，用以激励建功、威慑暴行；律，用以确定权属、平息纷争；令，用以指导民众使其明晓事务。

② 《新时代"枫桥经验"："定分"重在"止争"》，载最高人民法院网 2024 年 11 月 14 日，https://www.court.gov.cn/zixun/xiangqing/447501.html。

邓析

春秋末期
公元前 545 年—公元前 501 年

主要著述：《竹刑》
尊　　称：中国讼师鼻祖

Deng Xi

The Late Spring and Autumn Period
545–501 BCE

Major Work: *Written Law Carved on Bamboo Slips*
Honorific Title: The First Chinese Attorney

Life Story

Deng Xi, a native of the State of Zheng (now Xinzheng, Henan Province), was a leading figure of the School of Names and the initiator of ancient Chinese dialectics. He held the position of Grand Master when Zichan was the prime minister of the State of Zheng. As a pioneer in "advocating the shift from rites to law," Deng Xi opposed the "rule of rites" that safeguarded aristocratic privileges and proposed the "rule of law" instead. He argued, "Do not follow the ways of previous rulers, or treat law and discipline rite as immutable dogmas," emphasizing that laws should be made and executed based on the realities of the current society rather than blindly adhering to the ritual system of the Western Zhou Dynasty. Deng Xi "frequently criticized Zichan's administration," asserting that its unreconstructed reliance on rites and traditional laws was out of step with the demands of societal change. In "defiance of the authority," he privately revised the laws established by Zichan and carved them on bamboo slips, which became known as the "Written Law Carved on Bamboo Slips." Excelled in debate, Deng Xi not only taught the laws he had formulated to the masses but often offered legal assistance, always managing to present a convincing argument regardless of the stance he took. His ideas and actions angered the rulers of Zheng, who accused him of stirring up unrest and demagoguery. In 501 BCE, Deng Xi was executed by Si Chuan[i], then prime ruling minister of the State of Zheng, but his *Written Law Carved on Bamboo Slips* was adopted.

---

i Si Chuan was a descendant of Duke Mu of Zheng and a member of the Ji clan's Si lineage. He briefly served as prime minister of the State of Zheng, Si Chuan executed Deng Xi but adopted his *Written Law Carved on Bamboo Slips*. Si Chuan was killed by aristocrats due to intensified conflicts from the reforms the same year.

生平

邓析，春秋末期郑国（都城在今河南新郑）人，名家学派先驱人物之一，"名辩之学"早期实践者。子产执政时曾任郑国大夫，是"反礼倡法"先行者，否定维护贵族特权的"礼治"，倡导"法治"，主张"不法先王，不是礼义"，即不盲目效法先王，不奉西周礼制为圭臬，而要根据当前社会实际情况来制定和执行法律。邓析曾"数难子产之政"，认为子产政令仍固守礼制，不适应社会变革需求。因此他"不受君命"，私自改造子产刑书，书之于竹简，人称"竹刑"。邓析擅长辩论，不仅向众人讲授自己编制的法律，还常助人诉讼，无论立场如何皆能言之成理。郑国执政驷歂①（sì chuán）认为邓析欺惑民众、是非无度，而致民口喧哗、郑国大乱，遂"杀邓析而用其竹刑"。公元前501年，邓析被郑国执政者处死。

---

① 驷歂（sì chuán），郑穆公后裔，姬姓，驷氏，曾短暂任郑国执政。驷歂杀邓析却采用其《竹刑》，同年因改革激化矛盾 被贵族所杀。

Contributions As one of the pioneers of the Legalist School and the School of Names, Deng Xi championed the idea that "all decisions should be made according to the law," promoting the use of legal codes as the definitive basis for judgment and evaluation. He was known for his prowess in legal debate and logic, establishing himself as a trailblazer of debaters and initiating the trend of dialectic thoughts. Although Deng Xi was executed, *Written Law Carved on Bamboo Slips*, which embodied his legal philosophy, did not perish with him. Instead, they gained widespread acceptance and implementation in the State of Zheng.

Legacy Deng Xi was a distinguished thinker and reformist in the late Spring and Autumn Period, credited with advancing the concept of "legal terminology and principles." He pioneered the study of dialectics, earning recognition in the "Literature Records" in *The History of the Han Dynasty* as a representative figure of the School of Names. As a forerunner of both Legalist School and debaters, Deng Xi advocated that laws should evolve with society rather than remain bound by traditional ritual system. This perspective aligns with the fundamental principle that law should adapt to social changes effectively to

成就

作为名家、法家先驱之一，邓析主张"事断于法"，要以法律作为评价和判断事物的标准。他以擅长法律辩论和逻辑思辨著称，为辩论家先驱。邓析被处死后，代表其法律思想的"竹刑"却并未随之消亡，反而在郑国得到大力推广。

评价

邓析是春秋末期郑国思想家、改革家，首倡"刑名之论"，开创了名辩风气，被《汉书·艺文志》归类为名家学派代表人物之一。作为法家、辩论家先驱，他主张法律应适应社会发展，不应拘泥于传统礼制，这一观点符合法律应随社会变迁而不断发展完善，从而有效调整社会关系、维护社会秩序的根本宗旨。

regulate social relations and maintain social order. In addition, Deng Xi's "theory of dual possibilities" [i], which embodies a rudimentary dialectical thinking, resonates with the adversarial model in modern courtroom debate. For such reasons, he is celebrated as "the first Chinese attorney" in the history of China's legal system.

此外，邓析"两可说"[①]中蕴含的朴素辩证法思维，契合了现代法庭辩论中的对抗模式，因此在中国法制史上被称为"中国讼师鼻祖"。

---

[i] Theory of dual possibilities: Deng Xi's method of debate that embraced contradictory propositions. "Treat wrong as right and right as wrong with no fixed standards, making the permissible and impermissible change daily. He could justify any victory or condemnation at will." (From *Master Lü's Spring and Autumn Annals*) This method influenced the development of ancient Chinese logical thought and sparked later reflections on logic and debate.

① 两可说：指邓析提出的论辩方法，即对矛盾命题均采取认可态变，"以非为是，以是为非，是非无度，而可与不可日变。所欲胜因胜，所欲罪因罪"(《吕氏春秋》)。"两可说"对中国古代逻辑思想的发展产生了一定影响，引发后人对逻辑、辩论的认知。

邓析"两可说"

邓析不仅向人传授诉讼技法,更与涉讼者约定以案件大小收取衣物作为酬劳:"大狱一衣,小狱襦绔。"前来"献衣学讼者不可胜数",足见邓析的诉讼技巧和雄辩才能深受时人推崇。《吕氏春秋》中记载了一则故事:洧水泛滥,一位富人溺亡,有人打捞尸体后索以高价。富人家属求助邓析,邓析说:"不用担心,除你之外无人肯买。"于是富人家属不再急求尸体。卖尸者也焦急向邓析求助,邓析又巧辞回应:"姑且安心,除你之外对方再无可买之处。"时人评价其"操两可之说,设无穷之辞","以非为是,以是为非",说明邓析已在论辩技巧中融入了辩证法观念。

Deng Xi's "Theory of Dual Possibilities"

Deng Xi not only taught litigation techniques but also struck agreements with litigants, charging clothing as fees based on the case's complexity: "a robe for a major case, a tunic or trousers for a minor one." His exceptional rhetorical skills and expertise in legal disputes attracted countless individuals eager to trade garments for his teachings. *Master Lü's Spring and Autumn Annals* recounts a story about Deng Xi. A wealthy man drowned due to a flood in the Weishui River, and the person who retrieved his body demanded an exorbitant remuneration. The wealthy man's family sought Deng Xi's help, and he advised them, "Don't worry—no one but you will pay for the body." Reassured, they waited. Meanwhile, the seller grew anxious and turned to Deng Xi, who replied with equal finesse, "Be relaxed, you are their only option to buy the body." Critics of the time described Deng Xi as "manipulating arguments to suit both sides and crafting inexhaustible rhetoric," "turning false into true and true into false," illustrating his mastery of dialectical reasoning in debate.

楚庄王 茆门之法

茆门亦称雉门，为春秋时楚国宫门之一。为确保宫禁安全，楚庄王颁布了"茆门之法"，规定诸侯、大夫、公子入朝时，车皆不得行至茆门。一日，楚庄王急召太子，恰逢大雨庭中积水，太子遂驱车至茆门欲入。廷理依法阻止太子车驾，太子以君王急见为由，反欲驱赶廷理。于是廷理举殳（shū，古代的一种竹、木制成的兵器）击打太子马匹，打坏其车。太子恼怒，进宫后求楚庄王诛杀廷理。楚庄王问明来由，反赞廷理不违背法令、不攀附太子，为守法之臣，予晋爵二级，并告诫太子不可凌驾于法令之上。这一事件不仅彰显了楚庄王对法令的尊重，也反映出春秋时期成文法和"法不阿贵"精神在诸侯国的推行。

King Zhuang of Chu's Law of the Mao Gate

The Mao Gate, also known as the Zhi Gate, was one of the palace gates of the State of Chu during the Spring and Autumn Period. To ensure palace security, King Zhuang of Chu enacted the "Law of the Mao Gate," stipulating that no chariots of vassals, senior officials, or princes were allowed to approach the gate when entering court. One day, King Zhuang of Chu urgently summoned the Crown Prince during heavy rain, which had flooded the palace grounds. The Crown Prince drove his chariot to the Mao Gate and was lawfully halted by the court warden in charge. Citing the King's pressing summon, the Crown Prince attempted to force his way in. However, the warden beat his horse and damaged his carriage with a cudgel. Enraged, the Crown Prince complained to the King and demanded the warden be executed. After hearing the full account, King Zhuang of Chu praised the warden for adhering to the law and resisting favoritism, rewarding him with a promotion of two ranks. He also admonished the Crown Prince not to elevate himself above the law. This story highlights King Zhuang of Chu's commitment to upholding the law while reflecting the popularization of codified laws and the principle of "the law does not favor the nobility" among the feudal states during the Spring and Autumn Period.

子产铸刑书

公元前536年（春秋时期），郑国执政子产将法律条文铸刻于青铜鼎上，并公之于众，这一创举史称"铸刑书"。子产铸刑书首开中国历史上公布成文法之先河，摒弃了"临事议制，不豫设法"的临机裁决，革除了"刑不可知，则威不可测"的秘密法陋制，在中国法制史上具有开创性和奠基性意义。

Zichan's Casting of Code of Laws

In 536 BCE during the Spring and Autumn Period, Zichan, the prime minister of the State of Zheng, ordered legal statutes to be inscribed on bronze tripods and made public — a milestone event in Chinese legal history known as the "metal cast book of law." This groundbreaking act was the first recorded instance of codified law openly promulgated in China. It replaced the practice of ad hoc adjudication of cases without pre-established legal guidelines and abolished the secrecy of laws with the shortcoming of "If laws are obscure, their deterrent power remains unfathomable." Zichan's efforts laid a cornerstone in China's legal system.

李悝

战国初期
公元前 455 年—公元前 395 年

主要著述：《法经》《李子》
主要成就：编纂《法经》，推行变法

Li Kui

The Early Warring States Period
455–395 BCE

Major Works: *The Canon of Laws, Li Zi*
Major Contributions: Compilation of *The Canon of Laws*, implementation of legal reforms

Life Story　　Li Kui, also known as Li Ke in historical records, was born in the State of Wei during the Warring States Period. As a distinguished statesman and a key representative of Legalism, he once served as Counselor-in-chief of Zhongshan and Governor of Shangdi. Both places were located on the northwest border of the State of Wei, adjacent to the State of Qin, and he led his troops into battles against Qin multiple times. Afterward, Li Kui won the favor of Duke Wen of Wei, partly due to his mentor Zixia being a trusted minister of the Duke, and partly because his reform ideas precisely addressed the deep-rooted issues of Wei. Promoted to Counselor-in-chief of the State of Wei by the Duke, he spearheaded comprehensive reforms that rapidly strengthened Wei's national power.

Contributions　　Li Kui's reforms were groundbreaking in Chinese feudal history, exerting far-reaching influences on later generations. Politically, he dismantled hereditary aristocracy, establishing a meritocratic system with strict accountability. Economically, he abolished the well-field system, legalizing land privatization and transaction, which significantly boosted agricultural productivity. Militarily, he instituted standardized evaluations and restructured the army for efficiency. To consolidate the reforms, Li Kui compiled and applied The *Canon of Laws* by drawing on the codified laws of various states, which is composed of "Laws on Private Property Offence," "Laws on

生 平

　　李悝，史书又称"李克"，战国时魏国人，著名政治家，法家主要代表人物之一。曾任中山相、上地守，此两地皆位于魏国西北边境，与秦国接壤，李悝多次率军与秦国交战。后李悝得魏文侯青睐，一则因其师子夏为魏文侯股肱重臣，二则因其变法主张正中魏国痼疾。魏文侯遂擢李悝为魏国丞相，全面推行变法，魏国国力迅速强盛。

成 就

　　李悝变法是我国封建历史上具有开创意义的一次成功变法，对后世影响深远。变法在政治上，废止世袭贵族特权，选贤任能，赏罚分明；在经济上，废除井田制，允许土地私有和买卖，极大促进了魏国农业生产；在军事上，实行考核法，进行科学的军队编制。为巩固变法成果，李悝参考各国成文法，撷取其律法精华，编成《法经》并颁布推行。《法经》共六篇，分别

Violent Crime," "Laws on Trial," "Laws on Arrest," "Miscellaneous Laws," and "Laws on Sentence."

Regarded as a model of codified law of its era, the *Canon of Laws* marked the initial formation of a structured feudal legal framework and laid the foundation for the legal system of the feudal society. It deeply influenced legislative practices in the Warring States Period and beyond: Shang Yang used it as a blueprint for the *Laws of the State of Qin*; Xiao He expanded it into the *Nine Chapters Law*. From the Han Dynasty onward, successive legal codes all evolved from the Qin-Han framework, consistently incorporating its principles.

Legacy

Li Kui is hailed as the "Founder of Legalism," with his simultaneous emphasis on agriculture and rule of law exerting a tremendous influence on Shang Yang and Han Fei. His reforms ushered in a wave of reform in other states during the Warring States Period, including the famous ones pushed forward by Shang Yang and Wu Qi, who were inspired by the successful experiences of Li Kui. The legal principles, legal concepts, and codified structure established in the *Canon of Laws* by Li Kui not only pioneered the Chinese tradition of statutory compilation, but also laid the institutional foundation for building the ancient Chinese criminal law system.

为《盗法》《贼法》《网法》（也作《囚法》)《捕法》《杂法》《具法》，标志着封建社会法制体系的初步形成。《法经》不仅奠定了封建法制基本架构与准则，也对战国及后世立法产生了深远影响。 携《法经》入秦，以其为蓝本制定《秦律》；萧何在《法经》六篇基础上增补三篇，编成《九章律》；自汉代起，历朝法典皆在秦汉旧律基础上不断改进，且皆汲取了《法经》的核心原则。

评 价

李悝是法家学派重要奠基人，其"重农"与"法治"并举的思想对商鞅、韩非影响深远。李悝变法开战国时期各国变法之先河，后续广为人知的商鞅变法、吴起变法等，无不借鉴李悝变法成功经验。李悝在《法经》中所确立的法律原则、法律观念、法典体例，不仅开创了中国成文法典的编纂传统，也为构建中国古代刑法体系的框架和基础作出了贡献。

THE ORIGIN OF LAW

李离过杀伏剑

李离为春秋时期晋国掌管刑狱的最高长官,以公正无私和明察秋毫见称于世。一次,他却因误听案情而枉杀人命。李离悔愧不已,遂将自己拘禁,认为罪无可赦。晋文公宽慰他说:"官有贵贱,罚有轻重。此下级官员之过,非你之失。"李离说:"臣居官为长,不曾让高位于下属;受禄为多,亦不曾与下属分利。今过听杀人,实不应推诿罪责。狱官当循法办案,臣如今决断有误,枉杀人命,理应受刑。"最终他谢绝晋文公宽恕,伏剑自刎而死。司马迁将李离事迹写入《史记·循吏列传》,将其奉为严于律己、勇于担责的执法者典范,赞其曰"清廉自正""奉职循理"。

Li Li's Suicide After Ordering an Unjust Execution

Li Li, who served as the highest judicial officer of the State of Jin during the Spring and Autumn Period, was celebrated for his impartiality and keen discernment in handling cases. Yet, he once misjudged a case and caused the wrongful execution of an innocent person. Torn by remorse and guilt, Li Li threw himself into custody, deeming his error unforgivable. Duke Wen of Jin sought to console him, saying, "Officials have varying ranks, and penalties differ in severity. This mistake is the fault of your subordinates, not yours." But Li Li replied, "As the head of my office, I did not delegate my authority to others; as the beneficiary of higher pay, I did not share my earnings with them. Now, having erred in judgment and caused a wrongful death, I cannot shirk my responsibility. A judicial officer must handle cases according to the law. Since I failed in my duty and took an innocent life, I must face the penalty." Resolutely refusing Duke Wen of Jin's pardon, Li Li ended his own life with a sword. Hundreds of years later, Sima Qian regarded Li Li as a paragon of judicial personnel for his integrity and sense of duty, and recorded his story in the *Records of the Grand Historian* under "The Biographies of Exemplary Officials," extolling him as "upright and incorruptible" and "faithful to his duties."

商鞅

战国时期

约公元前 390 年—公元前 338 年

别　　称：卫鞅、公孙鞅、商君
主要著述：《商君书》
主要成就：推行变法，为秦统一六国打下基础

Shang Yang

The Warring States Period

c. 390–338 BCE

Alternate Names: Wei Yang, Gongsun Yang, Lord Shang
Major Work: *The Book of Lord Shang*
Major Contribution: Implementation of legal reforms that laid the groundwork for Qin's unification of China

Life Story

Shang Yang, a native of the State of Wei [i] (around Anyang, Henan Province), was surnamed Ji and belonged to the Gongsun Clan. He was thus also called Wei Yang and Gongsun Yang. He was enfeoffed with the Land of Shang and held the title of Lord Shang. Therefore, he was widely known as Shang Yang in history. A descendant of the royal clan of the State of Wei, Shang Yang was influenced by Li Kui and Wu Qi at a young age and developed a great passion for legal terminology and principles. He first served as a courtier in the household of Gongshu Cuo [ii], the Grand Councilor of the State of Wei. After Gongshu Cuo's passing, Shang Yang headed to the State of Qin carrying Li Kui's *Canon of Laws*, as he heard that Duke Xiao of Qin had an ambitious vision. Introduced by the Duke's trusted subordinate Jing Jian, he presented his reform strategies to the Duke, who was pleased upon hearing the proposals and appointed him as Left Chief Minister. After the initiation of reforms, Shang Yang was promoted to Da Liang Zao [iii] The reforms of Shang Yang quickly transformed Qin into the dominant power of the Warring States and paved the way for its future unification of China. In 338 BCE, Duke Xiao

生 平

商鞅，战国时期卫国（今河南安阳一带）人，姬姓，公孙氏，又称卫鞅、公孙鞅。后封于商，号商君，故史称商鞅。商鞅是卫国宗室后裔，少时受李悝、吴起影响，好刑名法术之学，后为魏国宰柜公叔痤家臣。公叔痤①死后，商鞅听闻秦孝公雄才大略，便携李悝《法经》前往秦国，经秦孝公亲信景监引荐，得见秦孝公，畅谈变法图强之策。秦孝公闻后大喜，遂任用商鞅为左庶长，开始变法，后升其为大良造②。商鞅变法使秦国迅速崛起，为秦一

---

[i] As "卫国" in Chinese, different from the subsequent State of We, a homophonous term written as "魏国", with which Gongshu Cuo was affiliated.

[ii] Gongshu Cuo: He was a counselor-in-chief of the State of Wei during the Warring States period, with Shang Yang as his household courtier.

[iii] Da Liang Zao: It was the highest official post and title concurrently held in the State of Qin from the reign of Duke Xiao of Qin until the Qin's conquest of the six other states. The holder of this position had control over both military and administrative affairs. Upon assuming this post, Shang Yang oversaw legal reforms while leading military expeditions. As Qin's bureaucratic system matured, Da Liang Zao eventually became an honorific title, stripped of its power.

① 公叔痤（gōng shū cuó）：战国时期曾任魏国相国，商鞅曾为其家臣。

② 大良造：秦孝公时期至秦灭六国前的秦国最高官职兼爵位，掌握军政大权。商鞅任此职后既掌管变法改革，又统领军队作战。后随着秦国官制完善，大良造逐渐变成象征性爵位，不再掌握实际权力。

of Qin passed away and was succeeded by his son, King Huiwen of Qin. The year also saw Shang Yang being framed for rebellion, hunted down, and executed.

Contributions   In the sixth year (356 BCE) and the twelfth year (350 BCE) of the reign of Duke Xiao of Qin, Shang Yang implemented two waves of reforms. Politically, he restructured Qin's household registration, military and nobility ranks, land distribution, administrative divisions, taxation system, standards of weights and measures, and folk customs, and enacted stringent legal codes. Economically, he prioritized agricultural development while curbing commerce and incentivizing farming and weaving. Militarily, he commanded the Qin army to reclaim territories of Hexi (regions west of the Yellow River). The reforms of Shang Yang progressively strengthened Qin in economy and military, setting the stage for its unification of China.

Legacy   Shang Yang was a pioneering statesman, reformer, and thinker of the Warring States Period, as well as a key representative of Legalism. His reforms, guided by the Legalist principle of "clarifying the law," ensured law as the highest principle of state governance, while dismantling privileges like "aristocrats were accorded lenient treatment in receiving penalties." Under his policies, Qin rapidly rose to prominence, surpassing

统六国奠定了坚实基础。公元前338年,秦孝公逝世,其子秦惠文王继位。同年,商鞅因被诬陷谋反而遭追捕,后被杀。

成 就

秦孝公六年(公元前356年)及十二年(公元前350年),商鞅先后两次推行变法。变法在政治上,改革秦国户籍、军功爵位、土地制度、行政区划、税收、度量衡及民风民俗,制定严格的律法;在经济上,重农抑商、奖励耕织;在军事上,商鞅作为统帅率领秦军收复河西。商鞅变法使秦国经济日渐强盛,战力日趋雄厚,为秦国统一六国奠定了基础。

评 价

商鞅是战国中期政治家、改革家、思想家,法家代表人物。他以法家"明法"态度推行改革,确立法律作为国家治理最高准则,废除"刑不上大夫"的礼治旧弊,秦国由此迅

all its rivals. The reforms of Shang Yang profoundly influenced the early development of Chinese legal systems and played a pivotal role in advancing China's historical trajectory toward great unification. His propositions, such as "punishment spares no rank," "strict enforcement of laws," and "laws must be clear and easily understood," also provided ideological reference for the development of later legal system.

速崛起，一跃成为战国七雄之首。商鞅变法对早期法律制度发展及中国历史大一统起到了重要推动作用，其"刑无等级""法令必行""法令明白易知"等主张也为后世法律制度发展提供了思想借鉴。

商鞅徙木立信

公元前 356 年，秦国左庶长商鞅为推行新法、取信于民，在法令颁布前，命人在国都南门立下三丈高木头一根，并公开悬赏："有能将此木椽搬至北门者，赏十金。"百姓诧异，无人敢尝试。商鞅随即将赏金提高至五十金。重赏之下，终于有人站出来搬动木椽置于北门，商鞅即刻兑现承诺，赏金如数支付，分文不少，此即"徙木立信"之典故。商鞅凭借"徙木立信"树新政之威，布"赏罚分明、法出必行"之道，此后，令行而变法始。

Shang Yang: Establishing Credibility by Rewarding People for Moving a Log

In 356 BCE, Shang Yang, Left Chief Minister of the State of Qin sought to gain public credibility before implementing his reforms. He placed a long log at the southern gate of the capital and announced a reward: "Anyone who moves this beam to the northern gate will receive a large amount of gold." The citizens were astonished, with none daring to act. Shang Yang then quintupled the reward. Enticed by the generous offer, someone finally stepped forward, carried the log to the northern gate, and was immediately paid the promised sum, not a single coin withheld. This historical episode, known as "Establish One's Credibility by Rewarding People for Moving a Log," enabled Shang Yang to establish the credibility of his administration and underscored his principle of keeping promises and enforcing laws with unwavering precision, marking the commencement of his institutional reforms.

荀况

战国末期

约公元前 313 年—公元前 238 年

别　　称：	荀子
主要著述：	《荀子》
主要成就：	儒法合流的先行者

Xun Kuang

The Late Warring States Period

c. 313–238 BCE

Alternate Name: Xunzi
Major Work: *Xun Zi*
Major Contribution: Forerunner of integrating Confucianism with Legalism

Life Story

Xunzi, born in the State of Zhao during the late Warring States Period, bore the given name Kuang and the courtesy name Qing. He journeyed to the State of Qi at the age of fifty (some accounts suggest fifteen) to pursue learning and became a lecturer at the Jixia Academy. By the reign of King Xiang of Qi, he was made "Zui Wei Lao Shi" [i] and "served as the Grand Councilor of the Jixia Academy three times." His travels once took him to the State of Qin, where he commended its governance under Shang Yang's reforms as "the pinnacle of governance." Xunzi also advised the State of Zhao on military matters and visited other states, such as Chu and Yan, to preach his political and legal philosophies. In his later years, Xunzi was invited by Huang Xie, the famous Lord Chunshen from the State of Chu, to take the position of Magistrate of Lanling (now Lanling County, Shandong Province). Following Lord Chunshen's assassination in 238 BCE, Xunzi was relieved of his post and passed away soon after.

Contributions

Xunzi integrated Confucian thoughts with Legalist philosophy, advancing a governance strategy that emphasized the fusion of rites and laws. He advocated codifying the essential tenets of rites into formal laws to achieve harmony between the two, asserting that "the foundation of governance lies in rites and legal punishment." In

生平

荀子,名况,字卿,战国末期赵国人。年五十（一说"年十五"）游学于齐,后在齐国稷下讲学。齐襄王时以他"最为老师"[①],曾"三为祭酒"。荀子曾入秦,对自商鞅变法以来的秦国政治评价很高,认为已达"治之至也"（治理国家的最高境界）。曾议兵于赵,并游历楚、燕等国,传播自己的政治和法治思想。晚年受楚国春申君黄歇邀请,任楚国兰陵（今山东兰陵县）令。公元前238年,春申君被杀,荀子罢官,居兰陵,不久去世。

成就

荀子在儒家思想基础上融合法家理念,提出"隆礼"与"重法"相结合的治国方略。他提倡将礼的基本原则法律化,以实现礼法统一,强调"治之经,

---

[i] Zui Wei Lao Shi (最为老师): This title was bestowed upon Xunzi during his lectures at the Jixia Academy, signifying his status as the most senior and venerable scholar. Here, "Lao Shi" denotes a highly respected academic leader, different from the contemporary meaning of "teacher".

① 最为老师:指荀子在齐国稷下讲学时被尊为最资深的学者。"老师"在此指德高望重的学术领袖,不同于现代教师含义。

Xunzi's view, "rites are the ultimate expression of humanity," while "law is the foundation of effective governance." He championed the creation and publication of written laws, insisting that "rewards must align with merit, and punishments must fit the crime" and opposing arbitrary enforcement. His vision of advocating rites and emphasizing law not only influenced the development of feudal legal systems since the Qin and Han dynasties but also influenced the philosophies of later Legalists like Han Fei and Li Si.

Legacy Xunzi was a seminal thinker of the late Warring States Period and a forerunner of integrating Confucianism with Legalism. He inherited and carried forward the Confucian notion of "rule of rites" while incorporating and refining the Legalist ideal of the "rule of law." His emphasis on balancing rites and laws not only offered the governance philosophy of "combining rites and laws, prioritizing virtue over punishment" for the feudal legal system after the Qin and Han dynasties, but provided historical inspiration for the contemporary integration of rule of law and rule of virtue in state governance.

礼与刑";"礼者，人道之极也"，"法者，治之始也"。他主张制定和公布成文法，要求"赏必当功，罚必称罪"，反对随意轻重。荀子礼法并重的主张对秦汉以后的封建法律制度产生了深远影响，也深刻影响了韩非、李斯等法家代表人物的思想和实践。

评 价

荀子是战国末期杰出思想家、儒法合流先行者。他继承和发展了儒家"礼治"思想，吸收和修正了法家"法治"理念，其礼法兼容并重的主张，不仅为秦汉以后的封建法律制度提供了"礼法合治、德主刑辅"的治国理念，也为当代法治与德治相结合的治国方略提供了宝贵的历史经验。

百人逐兔

《商君书·定分》及《慎子·内篇》通过"百人逐兔"故事，阐明了确定权利归属的必要性。一只兔子奔跑于田野，却有上百人争相追逐，并非因一只兔子足以供百人之需，而是因其归属尚未确定；成群的兔子堆积于市却无人擅取，并非人们不想获取，而是由于这些兔子权属明确。商鞅和慎到借此强调"定分止争"的重要性，认为通过法令明确各种权利归属是治国的关键，只有权属清晰，社会秩序才能维持，纷争才能得以平息。此论断不仅洞察了法律与社会秩序之间的深层联系，也揭示了法家"确权定分"的核心主张。

A Hundred People Chasing a Rabbit

The fable of "A Hundred People Chasing a Rabbit," as recounted in *The Book of Lord Shang* and *Shenzi*, illustrates the necessity of clearly fixing rights and duties. A rabbit darting across a field was chased by a hundred people — not because the rabbit could satisfy them all, but because its ownership was undecided. Conversely, heaps of rabbits in the marketplace remained untouched — not for lack of desire, but because their ownership was already determined. Through this story, Shang Yang and Shen Dao emphasized the importance of "fixing rights and settling disputes," asserting that delineating various rights through laws was fundamental to governance. According to them, only with clear ownership can social order prevail and disputes be resolved. This insight not only highlights the Legalist focus on property rights but also offers enduring perspectives on the interplay between law and social order.

THE ORIGIN OF LAW

韩非

战国末期
公元前 280 年—公元前 233 年

别　　称：韩非子、韩子
主要著述：《韩非子》
主要成就：法家思想集大成者，其思想指导秦始皇统一六国

Han Fei

The Late Warring States Period
280–233 BCE

Alternate Names: Han Feizi, Han Zi
Major Work: *Han Feizi*
Major Contribution: Foremost exponent of Legalist philosophy, whose ideas guided Qin Shi Huang (the first emperor of the Qin Dynasty) in unifying China

Life Story   Born into the aristocracy of the State of Han in Xinzheng (now Xinzheng, Henan Province) during the late Warring States Period, Han Fei was an adherent of Xunzi alongside Li Si. Despite the stammer that limited his articulation, Han Fei's literary prowess was unparalleled, to the extent that even. Li Si admitted being inferior. Facing the State of Han's declining power, Han Fei petitioned the King of Han multiple times, proposing reforms to strengthen the State. His advice, however, was ignored. Frustrated, Han Fei turned to writing, producing works such as *Solitary Indignation*, *Five Vermin*, *Inner and Outer Congeries of Sayings*, *Collected Persuasions*, *Difficulties in the Way of Persuasion,* and other political treatises, exceeding 100,000 Chinese characters in total. Though overlooked in the State of Han, Han Fei's essays caught the attention of Ying Zheng, the King of Qin, who then coerced the King of Han into sending Han Fei to his state through military threats. Nevertheless, after reaching Qin, Han Fei failed to gain a prominent position due to various reasons and ended up being imprisoned and killed.

Contributions   Han Fei integrated the doctrines of earlier Legalists, including Shang Yang, Shen Buhai, and Shen Dao, into a unified philosophical framework. He was the first to articulate the idea that "the law does not favor the nobility," advocating that "punishments must not spare high officials and rewards must not overlook commoners." His writings, primarily collected in *Han Feizi,* represented the pinnacle of

生 平

韩非，战国末期韩国贵族出身，生于新郑（今河南新郑市）。韩非与李斯同为荀子门下学生，他虽因口吃不善言辞，但文章出众，连李斯也自叹弗如。面对韩国之积弱，韩非屡次上书韩王，主张变法图强，但未被采纳。于是韩非退而著书，写出《孤愤》《五蠹》《内外储》《说林》《说难》等政治论文，凡十余万字。这些论文在韩国未能得到重视，却受到秦王嬴政赏识。秦王以派兵攻打韩国相威胁，迫使韩王令韩非入秦。韩非入秦后却因种种原因未得重用，反而被投进监狱处死。

成 就

韩非融会商鞅、申不害、慎到的法家思想于一体，首次明确提出"法不阿贵"，主张"刑过不避大臣，赏善不遗匹夫"，其著作主要收录在《韩非子》中。《韩非子》集法家思想之大成，宣扬

Legalist thoughts, advocating the integration of law, statecraft, and authority. His works laid the theoretical foundation for Qin's unification of China and the establishment of centralized rule in subsequent dynasties.

Legacy   Han Fei was an eminent thinker, philosopher, and essayist of the late Warring States Period and the foremost exponent of Legalist thoughts. His proposition of centralized autocratic monarchy emphasized that "the administrative power rests with subjects across the state, but the supreme authority must lie with the monarch." He stressed the strict enforcement of the law, asserting that "the law does not favor the nobility" and "punishments must not spare high officials." His trinity theory of "law, statecraft and authority" not only provided the ideological foundation for Qin's unification of China and establishment of the first centralized empire in Chinese history, but also profoundly influenced China's governance traditions for over two millennia thereafter.

法、术、势相结合的理论，为秦统一六国及后世的中央集权制度提供了理论依据。

评 价

韩非是战国末期杰出思想家、哲学家、散文家，法家思想集大成者。他提出君主专制中央集权的理论主张，主张"事在四方，要在中央"，强调法律的严格执行，做到"法不阿贵""刑过不避大臣"。其"法、术、势"三位一体的理论不仅为秦统一中国、建立历史上第一个中央集权的大帝国提供了思想武器，更对此后两千余年的中国治理传统产生了深刻影响。

张释之

西汉
生卒年不详

主要成就：提出"法者，天子所与天下公共"的法律思想

Zhang Shizhi

Western Han Dynasty
Dates of birth and death unknown

Major Contribution: The first in Chinese history to propose the legal philosophy of "the law is to be obeyed by the emperor and the entire populace alike"

Life Story

Zhang Shizhi, courtesy name Ji, was a native of Duyang (now Fangcheng, Nanyang, Henan Province) in the Western Han Dynasty. He rose through the ranks during the reign of Emperor Wen of Han, successively holding various positions, including Calvary Officer, Gate Traffic Control Officer, and Ordinary Grand Master. Eventually, he attained the prestigious role of Chamberlain for Law Enforcement[i]. Zhang earned his place in history through impartial law enforcement and forthright remonstrations. In cases where imperial edicts conflicted with the law, he upheld the principles of justice unwaveringly and counseled the emperor with candor. For instance, Zhang Shizhi once impeached the then Crown Prince, the future Emperor Jing, for "not dismounting at the Outer Palace Gate," insisting that "royals are subject to the same laws as commoners." Zhang Shizhi's uncompromising stance offended the Crown Prince, which led to his relegation to Grand Councilor of the Huainan Kingdom one year after Emperor Jing's ascent to the throne.

生 平

张释之，字季，西汉堵阳（今河南南阳方城）人。西汉文帝时历任骑郎、公车令、中大夫等，后官至廷尉①，以秉公执法、直言极谏闻名于世。当帝诏与法律发生抵触时，张释之能秉法不移，刚正劝谏。汉景帝为太子时，张释之曾弹劾其"过司马门不下车"，坚持"王子犯法与庶民同罪"。汉景帝即位一年后，张释之即被贬谪为淮南国国相。

---

[i] Ting Wei (Chamberlain for Law Enforcement): It was the highest judicial official in the central government during the Qin and Han dynasties. First established in the Qin Dynasty, this position ranked among the Nine Chamberlains and was in charge of all judicial and penal affairs across the empire. During the reign of Emperor Jing of the Western Han Dynasty, the title was changed to "Da Li," but Emperor Wu restored it to "Ting Wei." In the Eastern Han Dynasty and thereafter, the title alternated among "Ting Wei," "Da Li," and "Ting Wei Qing." After the Northern Qi Dynasty's bureaucratic system reform, the position was officially termed "Da Li Si Qing (Chief Minister of the Court of Judicial Review)," a title that remained in use until the Ming and Qing dynasties. [Based on *Cihai* (7th Edition)]

① 廷尉：是秦汉时期中央最高司法长官，始设于秦，位列九卿，执掌全国司法刑狱要务。西汉景帝时改称"大理"，武帝复名"廷尉"。东汉以降，或称"廷尉""大理""廷尉卿"。北齐改制后，统称"大理寺卿"。此制沿用至明清。[《辞海》（第七版）]

Contributions

Zhang Shizhi was the advocate in Chinese history for the legal concept that "the law is to be obeyed by the emperor and the entire populace alike" [i] and that "Chamberlain for Law Enforcement is the embodiment of justice; [ii] any bias of his will lead to inconsistencies in case handling and sentencing." Zhang adhered to the Legalist tenets of "the law does not favor the nobility" and "punishment spares no rank" while extending the Confucian values of "cultivating virtue and applying penalties with caution." On top of that, he also promoted the principle of "erring on the side of the defendant in cases of doubt" (i.e., prioritizing the rights of the accused when evidence is insufficient), opposing the misconduct of "allowing individual preferences or emotional volatility to dictate legal decisions." Zhang Shizhi, characterized by his unwavering commitment to justice and exemplary integrity in governance, was hailed as the paragon of a virtuous official, revered and honored for millennia.

Legacy

As a prominent Legalist scholar and jurist of the Western Han, Zhang Shizhi was renowned for his rigorous and

---

[i] The sentence underscores the law's universality and impartiality, indicating that the law is not a personal tool of the emperor but holds sway over him and all others, so the emperor is also obliged to conform to the law.

[ii] It means that the (Chamberlain for Law Enforcement) is a model for impartial justice; should he show any bias, the judicial practice of the entire empire will lose consistent standards.

成就

张释之是中国历史上首次明确记载提出"法者,天子所与天下公共"①"廷尉,天下之平也,一倾而天下用法皆为轻重"②的司法官员。他秉持法家"法不阿贵""刑无等级"的法治主张,继承儒家"明德慎罚"理念,倡导"罪疑者予民"(证据不足时应倾向保护被告人权利)的执法原则,摒弃"取舍在于爱憎,轻重由乎喜怒"的陋习。张释之以执法如山、从政廉明,被奉为理想循吏典范,为后世拥戴和称颂。

评价

张释之是西汉著名法学家、法官,以严明公正执法著称。他坚持以法律为准绳,不迎合君王

---

① 意思是:法律是天子和天下人所应共同遵守的。意在强调法律的普遍性和公平性,即法律并非天子的私人工具,而是对天子及天下所有人都具有约束力,天子也应当遵守法律。

② 意思是:廷尉是天下公正司法的表率,一旦出现偏斜,则全国的司法尺度将会失去统一标准。

just enforcement of the law. He upheld the law as the ultimate standard, refusing to pander to imperial desires or tolerate lopsided sentences influenced by personal bias. Historian Sima Qian praised him as one who "upheld the law without yielding to imperial will." His contemporaries praised him by saying that "Under Zhang Shizhi's tenure as Chamberlain for Law Enforcement, no one suffered injustice in the empire." Zhang Shizhi's ideas on the rule of law profoundly influenced later generations. His judicial ethos of "adjudicating with impartiality and deliberating laws with equitable leniency" established him as a model of official governance, and also provided valuable spiritual inspiration for contemporary society.

旨意，反对执法者依个人好恶而赏罚畸轻畸重，司马迁誉其"守法不阿上意"，时人赞曰"张释之为廷尉，天下无冤民"。张释之的法治理念深刻影响了后世，其以"处心公正，议法平恕"的司法品格被奉为吏治楷模，也为今天提供着宝贵的精神养分。

张释之不阿上意

汉文帝时，廷尉张释之以严守法度、不阿上意广受赞誉。一日，汉文帝乘辇出巡，行至中渭桥时，忽有一人从桥下奔出，惊动了御马。汉文帝命拘捕此人交廷尉治罪。张释之审问后奏报："此人违反清道戒严令，当处罚金。"汉文帝怒曰："此人惊吓了御马，幸亏此马脾性温和，若换作其他烈马，岂不致车毁人伤？廷尉竟只判处罚金?!"张释之对曰："法者，天子所与天下公共也，今法如此，若加重处罚，则法律无法取信于民。如今既交廷尉治罪，廷尉乃天下公平之象征，若有偏失，天下执法者则会随意轻重，百姓岂不无所适从？望陛下明察。"汉文帝沉默良久说："廷尉言之有理。"张释之在中国历史上明确提出"廷尉，天下之平也，一倾而天下用法皆为轻重"，是将中央司法审判机关定位为"天下司法准绳"的法律人物，体现了"以法为本""一断于法"的思想。时人赞其曰："张释之为廷尉，天下无冤民。"

Zhang Shizhi: Not Yielding to Imperial Will

Zhang Shizhi, the Chamberlain for Law Enforcement during the reign of Emperor Wen of Han, was widely praised for his unwavering commitment to justice, strict adherence to the rule of law, and integrity in not catering to imperial will. One day, while Emperor Wen was traveling by imperial carriage, a man suddenly darted out from beneath Zhongwei Bridge, startling the horses pulling the carriage. Emperor Wen ordered the man to be arrested and brought before Zhang Shizhi for sentencing. After interrogation, Zhang Shizhi reported, "This man violated the prohibition against obstructing the imperial procession and should be fined accordingly." Emperor Wen was furious and retorted "He startled the horses! Had they been of a fierce temperament, wouldn't it have resulted in the carriage being wrecked and the passengers being injured? And yet you suggest only a fine?!" Zhang replied firmly, "The law is to be obeyed by the emperor and the entire populace. The current statutes dictate a fine for such an offense. If we impose a harsher punishment, the credibility of the law will be undermined. This case has been assigned to me for sentencing. As the Chamberlain for Law Enforcement, I am the embodiment of justice. Should I waver, other enforcers of the law might act arbitrarily. Won't that leave the people in confusion? I implore Your Majesty to preserve the sanctity of the law." After a thoughtful pause, Emperor Wen conceded, "Your reasoning is sound." Zhang Shizhi was the initial advocate in Chinese history for the concept that "Chamberlain for Law Enforcement is the embodiment of justice; any bias of his will result in the arbitrary application of the law nationwide." Zhang Shizhi was figure to position the central judicial authority as the "criterion for judicial justice throughout the empire," manifesting the philosophies of "taking law as the fundamental principle" and "making decisions solely based on law." His contemporaries praised him by saying that "Under Zhang Shizhi's tenure as Chamberlain for Law Enforcement, no one suffered injustice in the empire."

汉文帝废肉刑

汉文帝十三年（公元前 167 年），齐地太仓令淳于意因罪将被施以肉刑，其幼女缇萦不忍见父亲受此极刑，遂随父赴京，并涕泣上书："死者不可复生，残者断肢不可复续，虽欲改过自新也再无机会，我愿作官婢以抵赎父亲刑罚。"汉文帝被缇萦的孝义感动，于是年五月颁布《除肉刑诏》，废除黥、劓、斩左右趾等肉刑，此举不仅标志着刑罚体系步入较文明阶段，也体现了对人性的尊重和对个体权利的保护。

The Abolition of Corporal Punishment by Emperor Wen of Han

In the 13th year of Emperor Wen of the Han Dynasty (167 BCE), Chunyu Yi, the granary official of Qi, was sentenced to corporal punishment for a crime. His young daughter Tiying, unable to bear the thought of her father being subjected to such brutal punishment, accompanied him to the capital and tearfully submitted a petition: "The dead cannot be revived, and severed limbs cannot be healed, leaving no opportunity for those who wish to repent. I am willing to serve in the palace as a bondmaid to commute my father's sentence." Emperor Wen was deeply moved by Tiying's devotion to her father and issued the *Edict on the Abolition of Corporal Punishment* in May of that year, eliminating corporal punishments such as tattooing, cutting off the nose or amputating the feet. This edict signified a move towards a more civilized penal system while demonstrating respect for human dignity and the protection of individual rights.

张汤审鼠

汉文帝时,长安丞之子张汤,幼而慧敏。一日,张父外出,命张汤照看家舍,回家后却发现家中的肉被老鼠叼去。张父因此责罚张汤,张汤不甘其责,怒而掘开鼠洞,擒住老鼠,将老鼠未食之肉一并找到。以残肉为证,张汤"自设公堂"对老鼠进行了一番控诉审问,并煞有介事地判处老鼠死刑。张父见张汤"审鼠"程序齐备,各类文书一应俱全,文辞似出自老狱吏之手,不禁大惊,遂开始教习张汤刑狱文书。汉武帝时,张汤官至御史大夫,执掌司法监察,位列九卿之首。其审鼠之事,见于《史记·酷吏列传》及《汉书·张汤传》中。体现了"程序正义"的生动启蒙。

Zhang Tang's Trial of the Mouse

Zhang Tang, son of an Aide of Chang'an Magistrate during the reign of Emperor Wen of the Han Dynasty, exhibited extraordinary intelligence at a young age. One day, Zhang Tang's father left home and instructed him to look after the household. Upon returning, the father discovered that some meat in their home had been stolen by a mouse and reprimanded Zhang Tang for that. Unwilling to accept the blame, Zhang Tang, in a fit of indignation, dug into the mouse hole, captured the culprit, and retrieved the uneaten portions of the stolen meat. With the remnants as evidence, Zhang Tang set up a makeshift courtroom where he interrogated, and charged the mouse, before sentencing it to death. He even went so far as to include a formalized trial procedure and detailed legal documentation. Astounded by the detailed procedure and paperwork, which mirrored that of seasoned legal clerks, Zhang Tang's father began training him in legal writing. During the reign of Emperor Wu of the Han Dynasty, Zhang Tang served as Censor-in-chief, the most prominent one among the Nine Chamberlains, wielding power over judicial and supervisory matters. His childhood trial of the mouse was recorded in the *Records of the Grand Historian* under "The Biographies of Ruthless Officials" and the *History of the Han Dynasty* under "Biography of Zhang Tang", vividly encapsulating the germination of "procedural justice."

杜预

魏末晋初
公元 222 年—公元 285 年

别　　称：杜武库
主要著述：《春秋左氏经传集解》《春秋释例》《律本》《杂律》《丧服要集》《女记》
主要成就：参与制定、注解《晋律》，兴建水利工程
谥　　号：成

Du Yu

Late Wei to Early Jin Dynasty
222–285

Alternate Name: Du Wuku
Major Works: *Annotations to Zuo Qiuming's Collected Commentaries on the Spring and Autumn Annals*, *Explanations and Examples of the Spring and Autumn Annals*, *Annotations to the Laws of Jin Dynasty*, *Miscellaneous Laws*, *Collections of Mourning Practices*, *Records on Women*
Major Contributions: Compiling and annotating the *Laws of Jin Dynasty*, overseeing water conservancy projects
Posthumous Title: Cheng

Life Story   Du Yu, courtesy name Yuankai, was a native of Duling in Jingzhao (now southeastern Xi'an, Shaanxi Province). Known for his extensive reading and prolific writings, Du was a polymath who had studied political economy, calendrical science, law, mathematics and historiography. He was given the nickname "Du Wuku (Wuku means armory)" by his peers, likening his vast knowledge to a full arsenal. Du Yu's father, Du Shu, was an upright and principled official whose clashes with powerful courtiers delayed Du Yu's entry into government service until his thirties. It was not until Sima Zhao rose to power that he was promoted to a position of importance. Du Yu performed several important tasks with great success: drafting and annotating the *Laws of Jin Dynasty*, initiating water conservancy projects, orchestrating a surprise attack on Xiling when commanding frontier defenses, and updating the calendar system. In 280, Du Yu was appointed by Sima Yan as the supreme commander of the expedition against Eastern Wu, ending the centuries-long division of the Three Kingdoms era. In early 285, Du Yu was transferred to the central government to serve as the Metropolitan Commandant. Unfortunately, he fell ill and passed away en route in Deng County at the age of sixty-three. Deeply mourning his loss, Sima Yan granted him the posthumous titles of General-in-Chief of the Southern Expedition, Commander Unequalled in Honor, and "Cheng".

生 平

杜预，字元凯，京兆杜陵（今陕西西安东南）人。自幼博览群书、勤于著述，对政经、历法、法律、数学、史学等皆有研究，时人赠"杜武库"别号，谓其博学多通，似武器库般无所不有。杜预之父杜恕忠正耿介，与朝中权臣不合，故杜预至三十多岁时仍未能入仕，直到司马昭执政后方受重用。他受命参与制定、注解《晋律》，多次出镇边关，其间，兴修水利，奇袭西陵，修订历法，成就卓著。公元280年，司马炎任命杜预为军事统帅征伐吴国，终结了三国以来的分裂局面。285年初，杜预被征调任命为司隶校尉，途中行至邓县时突然病逝，终年六十三岁。司马炎甚为哀悼，追赠征南大将军、开府仪同三司，谥号"成"。

Contributions

In 264, under Sima Zhao's directive, Du Yu led the drafting of the *Laws of Jin Dynasty* (also known as *Taishi Laws*). Building on the laws of the Han Dynasty and influencing those of the Tang Dynasty, it was the first to distinguish between *lü* (laws) and *ling* (ordinances). Du Yu was the first to bifurcate the "General Principles" section from the "List of Penalties", which made the general provisions of criminal law more comprehensive and set a precedent for later legal frameworks in imperial China. Afterward, Emperor Wu of Jin Dynasty (Sima Yan) commissioned Zhang Fei and Du Yu to annotate the *Laws of Jin Dynasty*. Their annotated version, known as the "Zhang-Du Laws," was granted the same authority as the original.

Legacy

Du Yu was erudite and versatile. Throughout his life, he achieved countless accomplishments in both political and military endeavors, excelling as a litterateur, jurist, and military strategist. Du Yu also oversaw many water conservancy projects that benefited the country and the people. He was the only man enshrined in both the Temple of Confucius and the Temple of Military God before the Ming Dynasty. Later generations honored him as "the preeminent figure of the Jin Dynasty." When compiling *Laws of Jin Dynasty*, he first proposed the

成就

公元264年，杜预受司马昭之命参与制定《晋律》（又称《泰始律》）。《晋律》上承汉律，下启唐律，最早区分了律（刑法制度）、令（规章制度）概念，首次从《刑名》中分出《法例》篇，刑律总则更加完备，对后世封建法律影响深远。后晋武帝又下令张斐和杜预对《晋律》进行注解，经张、杜二人注解后的《晋律》又称"张杜律"，与《晋律》具有同等效力。

评价

杜预是西晋时期博学多通的全能型人才，集法学家、军事家、文学家、水利专家于一身，文治、武功皆有建树，是明代以前唯一同时进入文庙、武庙的贤哲，被后世誉为"晋代第一流人物"。他在编订《晋律》时最早提出"律以正罪名，令以存事

legal classification theory that "statutes define crimes while ordinances regulate institutional practices," i thus laying the foundation for the maturity of ancient China's statute-ordinance legal system. His judicial doctrine of "unified legal authority" also resonates with the modern principle of judicial uniformity.

制"①的法律规范分类理论，为中国古代律令体系的成熟奠定了基础。其"法出一门"的司法主张，也与现代司法的统一性原则产生了历史共鸣。

---

i It means that statutes are the grounds for conviction and sentencing, and ordinances are instituted to regulate administrative affairs. This remark clarifies that legal documents, including laws and ordinances, serve distinct purposes respectively.

① 意思是：法律是用来定罪量刑的依据，而法令则是为了规范行政事务而设立。这句话用来说明律令等法律文件各有其不同用途。

刘颂

西晋

不详—公元 300 年

主要著述：《刘颂集》
主要成就：在中国历史上第一次明确提出封建法制"罪刑法定"原则
谥　　号：贞
封　　号：梁邹县侯

Liu Song

Western Jin Dynasty

? –300

Major Work: *Collected Works of Liu Song*
Major Contribution: First to define the feudal legal principle of "prescribed penalty for set crimes"
Posthumous Title: Zhen
Honorific Title: District Marquis of Liangzou

Life Story

Liu Song, courtesy name Ziya, was born in Guangling (now Yangzhou, Jiangsu Province) during the Western Jin Dynasty. Born into a renowned and influential family, he was the descendant of Liu Xu, Prince Li of Guangling, and the fourth son of Emperor Wu of Han. Liu Song earned distinction as a jurist and thinker during the Western Jin Dynasty. For four decades, Liu Song held key judicial and administrative roles in the central government, including Chamberlain for Law Enforcement and Minister of Personnel, advocating the judicial principle of strictly adjudicating cases based on the provisions of the law. After his death, Emperor Hui sent envoys to express condolences, granted his family a sum of 200,000 coins and court attire, and honored him with the posthumous title "Zhen."

Contributions

Liu Song held that cases adjudication should be based on the provisions of the law. According to him, rulings should defer to established principles of criminal law if no statute applied, and no crime could be declared in cases where neither statutes nor precedents provided guidance. He staunchly opposed judicial officials pandering to the whim of monarchs or bending laws to "fit subjective preferences," which led to arbitrary and unequal sentencing. Liu stated, "If existing laws are deemed flawed, they may be revised; otherwise, they must be enforced to the letter without perversion." Liu Song's adherence to strict law enforcement, uprightness, and impartiality led people to draw similarities between him and Zhang Shizhi,

生 平

刘颂，字子雅，西晋广陵（今江苏扬州）人。为汉武帝刘彻第四子、广陵厉王刘胥后代，是西晋时期著名法学家、思想家。任宫四十年间，刘颂长期负责中央司法、吏治，历任廷尉、吏部尚书等，力主严格根据法律条文断罪的司法原则。刘颂病逝后，惠帝派使者吊唁，赐钱二十万及朝服一套，谥号"贞"。

成 就

刘颂主张应以法律条文为依据严格依法断罪，无法律条文则应遵循刑名和法例，法律和名例都未有规定则不能定罪。他极力反对司法官吏迎合君主意志"看人设教"，以致撇开法律条文不用，量刑畸轻畸重。他说："若认为法律条文不尽妥当，可以修改；否则必须严格执行，不许枉法。"刘颂执法严明、耿直不阿、秉公处事，时人将他比作西汉廷尉张释之。

the Chamberlain for Law Enforcement of the Western Han Dynasty.

Legacy Liu Song was a distinguished jurist of the Western Jin and a prominent figure in Chinese history in practicing the law. He advocated the supremacy of law, insisting that even the monarchs were "bound by statutes." He was also the first to explicitly propose the principle of "a legally prescribed punishment for a specified crime." Contemporary legal scholar Zhang Jinfan remarked that "The legal philosophy of declaring crime based on statutes, represented by Liu Song during the Jin Dynasty, marked a significant advancement in Chinese legal history since the 'metal cast book of law', demonstrating that China's criminal law theory and system had reached the pinnacle of global standards for the time. While it cannot be deemed equal in terms of nature, scope, and stipulation, Liu's emphasis on strictly basing verdicts on codified laws aligned with the core principle of modern Western legal theories. Remarkably, China established this concept in the third century, predating similar Western developments by over a millennium. "

评 价

刘颂是西晋时期著名的法学家,也是我国历史上颇有影响力的法治实践家,他主张维护法律权威,即便贵为人君,也得"以律令从事",第一次明确提出了封建法制的"罪刑法定"原则。当代法学家张晋藩评价说:"晋代以刘颂为代表的思想家主张援法定罪,是铸刑书以来的重大成就,标志着中国刑法理论与制度达到当时世界最高水平。虽然它与近代西方罪刑法定主义的理论与实际在性质上、程度上、规定上还不能同日而语,但就基本原则即断罪以法律规定为准,则是一致的。中国在三世纪已经形成了鲜明的援法定罪的观点与律文,早于西方提出的罪刑法定一千余年。"

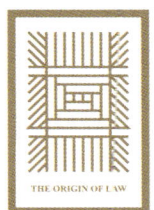

长孙无忌

隋唐

约公元 597 年—公元 659 年

主要著述：《唐律疏议》
主要成就：主持修订《唐律疏议》，为中华法系代表之作

Zhangsun Wuji

Sui and Tang Dynasties

c. 597–659

Major Work: *Tang Code*
Major Contribution: Overseeing the compilation of *Tang Code*, establishing the framework for criminal law in ancient China

Life Story   Zhangsun Wuji, courtesy name Fuji, was born in Luoyang, Henan Province. He came from the illustrious Zhangsun family and was the son of Zhangsun Sheng, the General of the Right Guard of the Sui Dynasty. Zhangsun Wuji developed a close bond with Li Shimin, Emperor Taizong of Tang, who later became his brother-in-law. During the reign of Emperor Taizong of Tang, he successively held prestigious posts such as General-in-chief Commanding Left Imperial Insignia Guard, Minister of Personnel, and Secretariat Director and was bestowed the title of Duke of Zhao. During the succession dispute, Zhangsun Wuji supported Li Zhi, the later Emperor Gaozong of Tang. Afterward, he was appointed as an assisting minister for the future monarch and granted the position of Grand Commandant and Cooperating with Third Rank Officials of the Secretariat-Chancellery ⅰ. After Emperor Taizong's decease, Zhangsun Wuji continued to assist Emperor Gaozong. However, his opposition to Wu Zetian's becoming Empress led to false accusations of rebellion. Stripped of all titles and exiled to Qianzhou, Zhangsun Wuji was forced to commit suicide. In the first year of the Shangyuan era (674), Emperor Gaozong reinstated Zhangsun Wuji's titles and allowed his remains to be interred at Zhao Mausoleum.

ⅰ Cooperating with Third Rank Officials of the Secretariat-Chancellery: A title for Grand Councilors in the Tang Dynasty. It was bestowed upon officials who, though not the chiefs of the Three Departments (Secretariat, Chancellery, and the Department of State Affairs), were involved in central governmental decision-making.

生 平

长孙无忌，字辅机，河南洛阳人。出身于河南长孙氏，是隋朝右骁卫将军长孙晟之子。自幼与唐太宗李世民关系密切，后来成为姻亲。历任左武侯大将军、吏部尚书、中书令等，封赵国公。在立储之争时长孙无忌支持唐高宗李治，后被任命为顾命大臣，授太尉、同中书门下三品①。唐太宗死后，长孙无忌继续辅佐唐高宗李治，后因反对立武则天为后，被诬陷谋反，削爵流放黔州，最终被迫自缢而死。上元元年（公元674年），唐高宗追复长孙无忌官爵，允许将其灵柩陪葬于昭陵。

---

① 同中书门下三品：是唐朝的一种宰相职衔，用于授予非三省（中书省、门下省、尚书省）长官但参与中枢决策的官员。

Contributions

Upon Emperor Taizong's ascension to the throne, Zhangsun Wuji, together with Fang Xuanling and others, was tasked with compiling *The Law in Zhenguan Time of Tang Dynasty* to build a legal framework for the Tang Dynasty. In the second year of the Yonghui era (651), under Emperor Gaozong, Zhangsun Wuji led the compilation and promulgation of *The Law in Yonghui Time of Tang Dynasty* based on *The Law in Zhenguan Time of Tang Dynasty*. To address inconsistencies in judicial interpretations of the new law code between central and local courts, Emperor Gaozong ordered detailed commentary on its provisions. These annotations, known as *lü shu* ("code commentary"), were appended to the legal text and promulgated in the fourth year of the Yonghui era (653) as *Commentary on the Law Codes in Yonghui Time*, which was called *Tang Code* by later generations. This work integrated the legislative achievements of earlier dynasties into a coherent system while formalizing the practice of attaching commentary to legal statutes, to become the most influential feudal legal code in Chinese history. Its essence was widely adopted by neighboring states such as Korea, Japan, and Vietnam, cementing its role in the global legal system.

成就

唐太宗李世民即位后,为完善法律规范,命长孙无忌、房玄龄等人修订完成《贞观律》,奠定了唐代律法基础。唐永徽二年(公元651年),唐高宗李治命长孙无忌等人以《贞观律》为蓝本,修订并颁布《永徽律》。后鉴于中央和地方在审判中对《永徽律》条文解释不一,李治又下令对《永徽律》进行逐条详解,解释内容被称为"律疏",附在相应律文之下,于永徽四年(公元653年)颁行,时称《永徽律疏》,后世称为《唐律疏议》。《唐律疏议》承袭魏晋南北朝以来的立法成就,开创了律条之后附以注疏的法典体例,不仅是中国历史上最具影响力的封建法典,其法理精髓还广泛传播到朝鲜、日本、越南等亚洲各国,在世界法律体系中占有一席之地。

Legacy As a founding statesman of the Tang Dynasty and a distinguished politician, Zhangsun Wuji served under three monarchs and held the post of Grand Councilor for over three decades. His achievements extended beyond political governance and military strategy to remarkable contributions to the legal field. *Tang Code* overseen by him fused Confucian ideals of law and discipline rite and set a precedent of "giving commentaries to laws after they have been enacted to enforce them" to promote unified judicial standards. Zhangsun Wuji's efforts facilitated the Tang Dynasty's political and economic advancement and the perfection of its legal system while also exerting a far-reaching influence on the legislation of subsequent eras and adjacent nations, underscoring the brilliant feats of Chinese legal civilization in the annals of world legal systems. His legal contributions are deeply woven into the fabric of the Chinese legal tradition, providing invaluable legal cultural resources for contemporary legal reform.

评 价

长孙无忌是唐代著名政治家、法学家,任宰相三十余载,不仅政绩斐然,更以法律成就彪炳史册。其主持修订的《唐律疏议》融入儒家礼法精神,开创了"疏在律后,律以疏存"的立法先河,不仅为唐代政治经济发展及法律制度完善作出了贡献,也对后世及周边国家立法影响深远,彰显了中华法治文明在世界法治史上的卓越地位。其法治成就已融入中华法系脉络,为今天的法治建设提供着宝贵的法律文化资源。

唐太宗览图禁杖

贞观四年（公元 630 年），《明堂针灸图》官修已毕，呈唐太宗御览。唐太宗观此图发现，人体五脏六腑之经络孔穴皆附于脊背，针灸时若有偏差不慎，即有损伤人体之虞。由是联想到笞杖之刑要击打犯人脊背，则更易损伤脏腑，甚至致人死命。而笞、杖已为轻刑，轻刑便要伤及性命，实非所宜。于是唐太宗下诏，命问刑衙门今后不得用笞杖刑具击打犯人背部。此诏一出，免毙杖下者众。此举体现了唐代法律蕴含的"用刑持平""务在宽简"等宽仁慎刑理念，反映出唐律与儒家思想的制度化融合。

Emperor Taizong of Tang Banned Caning After Reviewing the Acupuncture Diagram

In the fourth year of the Zhenguan era (630), the official compilation of the *Mingtang Acupuncture Diagram* was completed and presented to Emperor Taizong of Tang for review. While examining the diagram, Emperor Taizong noted that the meridians and acupoints corresponding to the vital organs of the human body were concentrated along the spine. A slight error in acupuncture could potentially harm the organs and jeopardize the patient's life. This observation made him reflect on the judicial use of caning, a punishment that involved striking a convict's back with rods or canes. If acupuncture carried such risks, caning could damage the internal organs more easily or even cause death. Considering that caning was categorized as a minor punishment, its life-threatening consequences seemed fairly inappropriate. Therefore, Emperor Taizong issued an edict forbidding the use of flogging instruments on the backs of convicts, which spared numerous individuals from death under corporal punishment. Emperor Taizong's approach to governance, which was characterized by "leniency and a particular focus on humane practices in criminal justice," reflected the institutionalized integration of the Tang Dynasty's laws and Confucianism.

唐太宗与"五复奏"

死刑复奏制度萌芽于汉，发展于南北朝，至隋朝时已确立"三复奏"制度，即死刑案件需三次奏报皇帝批准方可执行。贞观五年（公元631年），大理寺丞①张蕴古遭弹劾，唐太宗盛怒之下下令斩杀张蕴古。事后，唐太宗追悔莫及，认为张蕴古罪不当死。为防止类似未暇审思而错杀情形发生，唐太宗将京师地区死刑改为"五复奏"，即便已经御笔勾决，仍须完成全部复奏程序。此举强化了死刑复奏的程序正义，体现了唐代法律的"慎刑"理念。

Emperor Taizong of Tang and the "Five-Review System"

The system of reviewing death penalty cases originated during the Han Dynasty, developed further in the Northern and Southern Dynasties, and became institutionalized in the Sui Dynasty as the "Three-Review System," which mandated that all death penalty cases should be submitted to the Emperor three times for approval before the execution. In the fifth year of the Zhenguan era (631), Zhang Yungu, the then Assistant Minister of the Court of Judicial Review (Dalisi) ⅰ, was impeached. In anger, Emperor Taizong ordered his execution. Afterward, consumed with remorse, Taizong acknowledged that Zhang's crime did not warrant such a severe punishment. To avoid similar instances of hasty decisions leading to wrongful executions, the Emperor extended the "Three-Review System" to the "Five-review System." Even after the emperor's final endorsement, the sentence still had to undergo five rounds of review, which reinforced procedural justice in capital punishment and reflected the Tang legal philosophy of "prudent punishment."

---

① 大理寺为北齐始设的中央最高审判机构（隋唐时与刑部、御史台并称"三法司"），长官称"大理寺卿"，"大理寺丞"为其属官（唐代定员六人），辅佐大理寺卿审理案件。

ⅰ Da Li Si (the Court of Judicial Review), established in the Northern Qi Dynasty, was the supreme central judicial institution (in the Sui and Tang Dynasties, it was one of the "Three Judicial Offices" alongside the Ministry of Justice and the Censorate). Its chief official was known as "Da Li Si Qing (Chief Minister of the Court of Judicial Review)", while "Da Li Si Cheng (Aides of Court of Judicial Review)" acted as his subordinate (with a set number of six in the Tang Dynasty), assisting in adjudicating cases.

包拯

北宋

公元 999 年—公元 1062 年

别　　称：	包公、包龙图、包青天
主要著述：	《包孝肃公奏议》
谥　　号：	孝肃

Bao Zheng

Northern Song Dynasty

999–1062

Alternate Names: Bao Gong, Bao Longtu, Bao Qingtian

Major Work: *Collection of Bao Zheng's Memorials to the Throne*

Posthumous Title: Xiaosu

Life Story

Bao Zheng, courtesy name Xiren, was a prominent statesman of the Northern Song Dynasty. He was born in Hefei, Luzhou (now Hefei, Anhui Province). In 1027, Bao Zheng was admitted as a Jinshi (Presented Scholar). He subsequently took on various posts, including Investigating Censor, Auxiliary Academician of Dragon Diagram Hall, Governor of Kaifeng, Vice Censor-in-chief, and State Finance Commissioner. Bao Zheng was known for his unyielding stance, incorruptibility, impartiality, and astute judgments in court. Never fawning over the bigwigs, he always stood up for the common people, which earned him the laudatory titles of Bao Qingtian and Bao Gong. In the sixth year of the Jiayou era (1061), Bao Zheng was appointed Vice Military Affairs Commissioner, yet he died of illness in the following year (1062) at sixty-four. Emperor Renzong of Song Dynasty attended his funeral in person and canceled the court sessions for a day as a gesture of mourning. Emperor Renzong also honored him posthumously with the rank of Minister of Rites and the title of "Xiaosu." Bao Zheng's legendary fairness and uprightness have been eulogized for generations through operas, story-telling script novels, and folklore, making him a lasting symbol of justice, integrity, and wisdom in Chinese culture.

生平

包拯，字希仁，庐州合肥（今安徽合肥）人，北宋名臣。天圣五年（1027年）登进士第，历任监察御史、龙图阁直学士、权知开封府、御史中丞、三司使等职。包拯立朝刚毅、廉洁公正、铁面无私，且英明决断、不附权贵，敢于替百姓鸣不平，故在民间有"包青天""包公"之美名。嘉祐六年（1061年）任枢密副使，次年（1062年）病逝，年六十四。宋仁宗亲临吊奠，并辍朝一日，追赠其为礼部尚书，谥号"孝肃"。包拯的事迹和轶闻被民间世代传颂，其公正磊落的人物形象通过戏曲、话本、小说等形式广为流传，成为中国文化中正义、光明、智慧的象征。

Contributions

Bao Zheng was distinguished by his astute and upright manner in settling lawsuits and enforcing the law. Despite the challenges of governing Dongjing (now Kaifeng), home to members of the imperial family and aristocrats, he showed no favoritism, disciplined the officials, and pled for the people, "gaining a formidable fame that resonated throughout the city." He valued the principle of "governing with the scales of law" and the importance of legal stability, opposing the arbitrary approach of "enacting or repealing laws at a whim." On the political front, Bao Zheng supported the advancement of capable and honest officials, expecting Emperor Renzong to adopt a clear-cut stance in rewarding or punishing those who deserved it and appoint upright officials to enforce the law. He deemed that "loyal and upright ones should be rewarded for their merits, while those who are treacherous and wicked must be punished for their crimes." Bao Zheng also empathized deeply with the plight of the people, proposing policies such as "reducing taxes, easing corvee labor, and alleviating famine." He recommended "streamlining bureaucracy, downsizing the military, curbing unnecessary construction, and promoting frugality." These reforms and proposals significantly influenced the Northern Song Dynasty and left a rich legacy of legal and political thought that continues to inspire.

成就

包拯以断讼执法、明敏正直著称。面对东京（今开封）众多皇亲国戚，他不徇私情，整饬吏治，为民请命，"威名震动都下"。他主张"以法律提衡天下"，强调法令的稳定性，反对"一言立法，一言废法"。政治上他举贤任能，期望仁宗赏罚分明，任用正直的官员执掌法律，"忠直者有功则赏，邪佞者有罪必罚"。他体察百姓疾苦，提出"薄赋敛，宽力役，救荒馑"，并主张"减冗吏、减冗兵、减修建、省奢侈"，这些举措和谏议不仅在当时产生了重要影响，也为后世留下了宝贵的法治思想和政治遗产。

Legacy   Bao Zheng stands out in Chinese history as both a "staunchly upright minister" and a quintessential representative of officials free from corruption. His legal philosophy was rooted in people-oriented thoughts, highlighting that "the people are the foundation of the nation." He advocated for legislation that "balanced societal and individual needs" and focused on the welfare of the people. His judicial principle of "taking the law as the yardstick" and his wisdom in handling cases with keen perception and decisive judgment have elevated the figure of "Bao Qingtian" beyond historical confines, rendering him a symbol of justice in traditional Chinese legal culture, representing "a just legal system that guarantees people's well-being," and also embodying humanity's enduring quest for fairness and justice.

评 价

包拯是中国历史上著名的"劲正之臣",也是清官廉吏的典型代表。他的法律理念以民本主义为出发点,强调"民者,国之本也",主张立法应"公私利济",关切民生利益。其"以律为绳"的司法原则和明察善断的办案智慧,使得"包青天"这一人物形象超越历史范畴,成为中华传统法律文化中"法正民安"的正义符号,也寄托了人们对公平正义的永恒追求。

宋慈

南宋
公元 1186 年—公元 1249 年

主要著述：《洗冤集录》
主要成就：开创"法医鉴定学"
尊　　称：法医学之父、世界法医学奠基人

Song Ci

Southern Song Dynasty
1186–1249

Major Work: *Collected Cases of Injustice Rectified*
Major Contribution: Founder of "Forensic Identification"
Honorific Titles: Father of Forensic Medicine, Pioneer of Global Forensic Science

Life Story

Song Ci, courtesy name Huifu, was a native of Jianyang, Fujian (now Nanping, Fujian Province). Born into an official family, his lineage could be traced back to a renowned Tang-Dynasty Grand Councilor named Song Jing. His father, Song Gong, once served as the Prefectural Judge of Guangzhou in the Southern Song Dynasty, supervising criminal investigations in the Private Secretariat of the Military Commissioner. In his childhood, Song Ci received education from Wu Zhi, a disciple of the great philosopher Zhu Xi. He was admitted to the Imperial College at twenty and became a Jinshi (Presented Scholar) in the tenth year of the Jiading era (1217). Early in his career, Song Ci participated in several military campaigns to quell rebellions, earning high praise from his commanders for his exceptional courage and loyalty, with one noting that he "surpassed even military officers." Due to his military merits, Song Ci was promoted to Judicial Commissioner of Guangdong. He conducted cases with great scrutiny and placed particular emphasis on on-site inspections of criminal and homicide cases. Within eight months, he successfully resolved over 200 backlogged cases accumulated over the years in Guangdong. Due to his performance, he was later transferred to other prefectures like Jiangxi and Hunan. In the winter of the seventh year of the Chunyou era (1247), Song Ci completed his masterpiece—*Collected Cases of Injustice Rectified*. In the following winter, he was appointed as Auxiliary Academician of the Hall for Treasuring the Heritage. Soon, in 1249, he was promoted to Auxiliary Academician

生平

宋慈,字惠父,福建建阳(今属福建南平)人。出身于官宦家庭,其祖上为唐朝著名宰相宋璟。父宋巩曾任南宋广州节度推官,在节度使幕府掌管刑狱。宋慈幼年受业于朱熹弟子吴稚门下,二十岁入太学,嘉定十年(1217年)中进士。入仕途之初即参与数次平叛战争,显示出过人的军事才能,主帅赞其"忠勇过武将矣"。因屡立军功,宋慈被提拔任用为广东刑狱,他办案详审,特别重视刑命案件的现场检验,八个月间便连断积年累案二百余件,后又往江西、湖南等地任刑狱吏。淳祐七年(1247年)冬,宋慈完成传世名著《洗冤集录》;淳祐八年(1248年)任宝谟阁直学士;翌年,升任焕章阁直学士、广州知州与广东经略安抚使,宋慈到任不久后忽患头晕病,于同年三月初七逝于广州官寓,终年六十四岁。

of the Hall for Brilliant Literature, Prefect of Guangzhou, and Military Commissioner of Guangdong. Shortly after assuming office, Song Ci unexpectedly fell ill with dizziness and expired in his official abode in Guangzhou on the seventh of the third month in the Chinese calendar of 1249, aged sixty-four.

Contributions

Throughout his two decades of career in judicial and criminal investigation, Song Ci laid stress on evidence collection and thorough examinations. He personally inspected complex cases, accumulating invaluable forensic experience. Building on the work of his predecessors and his practice, he authored *Collected Cases of Injustice Rectified*, systematically documenting methods for wound inspection, autopsy, bone examination, determination of death and injury, identification of poisons, analysis of evidence, as well as first-aid techniques and antidote prescriptions. The cases collected in the book demonstrated Song Ci's rational, evidence-based approach and prudent forensic techniques. *Collected Cases of Injustice Rectified* is the world's first systematic treatise on forensic medicine, predating *De Relationibus Medicorum Libri Quatuor* by the Italian physician Fortunati Fidelis, the founder of forensic science in Europe, by over 350 years. The book has been translated into English, French, German and other languages. Joseph Needham, the renowned sinologist and British biochemist and historian of science, highlighted in Science and Civilisation in China that "*Collected Cases of Injustice Rectified*, written in 1247, was the first systematic book

成 就

宋慈在二十余年司法刑狱生涯中，注重调查取证，积累了丰富的法医学经验。他在总结前人经验基础上，结合自身实践著成《洗冤集录》，系统记载了验伤、验尸、检骨、死伤鉴别、毒物分辨、证据分析，以及急救法、解毒药方等内容，书中案例展示了宋慈理性的实证态度和审慎的检验技术。《洗冤集录》是世界第一部法医学专著，比欧洲法医学奠基人、意大利医生菲德里所著《医生的报告》早三百五十余年，曾先后被译为英、法、德等文字。著名汉学家、英国生物化学和科学史学家李约瑟在《中国科学技术史》中特别写道："《洗冤集录》比欧洲最早的法医学著作早三个半世纪，中国这一成就的重要性显而易见。"

of forensic medicine in the world, being three and a half centuries earlier than anything of the kind in Europe. The importance of this Chinese achievement is obvious."

Legacy Song Ci was an outstanding forensic scientist in ancient China, known as the "Father of Forensic Medicine." His masterpiece, *Collected Cases of Injustice Rectified*, stands as the earliest systematic forensic monograph in the world, which was widely applied in judicial examinations in ancient China and left a lasting impact on the development of forensic medicine in China and worldwide. Song Ci's evidence-base judicial inspection system serves as a bridge between ancient judicial wisdom and modern forensic medicine. This system continues to shine with the radiance of rationality.

评 价

　　宋慈是我国古代法医学奠基人，被称为"法医学之父"。其著作《洗冤集录》是世界第一部系统性的法医学著作，不仅被广泛应用于我国古代司法检验工作，也对世界法医学发展作出了巨大贡献。宋慈构筑的以实证为核心的司法检验体系架起了古代司法智慧与现代法医学之间的桥梁，至今仍闪耀着理性的光芒。

王阳明
爱民如子

王阳明是明代杰出思想家、军事家、政治家,被誉为立德、立功、立言"三不朽"的圣人。治理地方时,王阳明深谙道德教化有助于法律的施行,因此不能仅靠刑罚威慑,而应以劝导、教育为先。他说:"若使果然视民如己子,亦安忍不施教诲劝勉,而辄加棰楚鞭挞",体现出"仁者爱人"的民本理念。王阳明之治,不惟以法,更秉承"和为贵"理念,以德化人,其所治地方民风渐趋敦厚,礼让之风盛行。

Wang Yangming: Governing with Compassion

Wang Yangming was a distinguished philosopher, military strategist, and statesman of the Ming Dynasty, revered as a sage accomplishing the "Three Immortalities" of virtue, achievement, and thought. In his approach to local governance, Wang deeply understood that moral education facilitated the effective implementation of laws. He believed that governance should not rely solely on punitive measures but should prioritize guidance and education. He once remarked, "If an official regards the people as his children, how could he cruelly skip education and encouragement, rushing instead to impose whippings and beatings?" This sentiment reflects his profound care for the people and his conviction that moral guidance should take precedence over punishment. Wang's governance integrated law with virtue cultivation. Under his administration, the regions he governed grew harmonious, with an ethos of decency and courtesy becoming the prevailing norm.

黄宗羲

明末清初

公元 1610 年—公元 1695 年

别　　称：梨洲先生
主要著述：《南雷文定》《明儒学案》《宋元学案》《明夷待访录》
尊　　称：中国启蒙思想家

Huang Zongxi

Late Ming to Early Qing Dynasties
1610–1695

Alternate Name: Lizhou Xiansheng
Major Works: *Essays of Huang Nanlei, Matters of Learning Among Ming Neo-Confucians, Matters of Learning Among Ming Song-Yuan Confucians, A Plan for the Prince*
Honorific Title: Father of Chinese Enlightenment

Life Story

Huang Zongxi, courtesy name Taichong and ideal-expressing name Nanlei, was a native of Yuyao, Zhejiang Province. He was also known as Lizhou Xiansheng. His father, Huang Zunsu, was a prominent scholar of the Donglin Faction, yet fell victim to Wei Zhongxian's persecution and died in prison. In the first year of the Chongzhen era (1628), nineteen-year-old Huang Zongxi traveled to the capital to seek justice for his father, carrying a dagger concealed in his sleeve. During the hearing, he lashed out at Wei Zhongxian's supporters with the dagger and mourned his father publicly at the prison gate, earning widespread admiration for his courage. Even Emperor Chongzhen lauded him as the "loyal son of a virtuous official." After returning home, he devoted himself to scholarly pursuits, studying under Liu Zongzhou, a great Confucian scholar of the late Ming Dynasty, and embracing the Jishan School [i]. When Qing forces advanced south, Huang organized the resistance "Shizhong Battalion" for half a year. In the tenth year of the Shunzhi era (1653), he returned to his hometown to teach and write in seclusion, steadfastly refusing all appointments from the Qing government. Huang Zongxi passed away on August 12, 1695, the 34th year of Emperor Kangxi's reign, aged eighty-six.

---

i　Jishan School: A Confucian philosophical system established by Liu Zongzhou, a prominent Confucian scholar of the late Ming Dynasty. As Liu Zongzhou taught for many years at Jishan in Shaoxing and was widely recognized as "Master Jishan," the school was thus named. His theory emphasized "restraining in privacy" and "sincerity of will," leaving a lasting impact on his students, including Huang Zongxi.

生 平

黄宗羲，字太冲，号南雷，人称梨洲先生，浙江余姚人。其父黄尊素是"东林党"名士，被魏忠贤所害，冤死于诏狱。崇祯元年（1628年），十九岁的黄宗羲"袖长锥"入京讼冤，审讯时以锥击刺魏党余孽，哭祭于诏狱中门，浩气震动内外，崇祯帝叹其为"忠臣孤子"。归乡后发愤读书，师从晚明大儒刘宗周，得蕺山之学①。清兵南下时，组织"世忠营"武装抵抗达半年之久。顺治十年（1653年）返回故里课徒授业，屡拒清廷征召，隐居著述。康熙三十四年（1695年），黄宗羲与世长辞，终年八十六岁。

---

①　蕺（jí）山之学：指晚明大儒刘宗周创立的儒学思想体系。因刘宗周长期在绍兴蕺山讲学，世称"蕺山先生"，故得名。其学说以"慎独""诚意"为核心，对黄宗羲等弟子影响深远。

Contributions From a "people-oriented" perspective, Huang Zongxi denounced the autocratic monarchy and advocated legislation for the public good to replace "the law designed solely for the interests of the imperial family" with "the law of the people," putting forth the people-oriented idea that "the people are the masters of the country, and the monarch is but a guest." His "new people-oriented thought" surpassed the traditional Confucian paradigm of "prioritizing the people, caring for the people, and pleading for the people" within the framework of monarchical despotism, advancing toward modern concepts of law and democracy. A polymath, Huang Zongxi made lasting contributions across fields as diverse as Confucian classics, history, philosophy, astronomy, calendrical calculations, music, Buddhism, Daoism, agriculture, and handicraft. His extensive writing scomprised over fifty works and over 300 volumes, the influential ones include *Essays of Huang Nanlei*, *Matters of Learning Among Ming Neo-Confucians*, *Matters of Learning Among Ming Song-Yuan Confucians*, and *A Plan for the Prince*.

Legacy Huang Zongxi is widely regarded as one of China's most distinguished Enlightenment thinkers, as well as an accomplished philosopher, historian, and litterateur. His system of thought prioritized "addressing societal needs and practical matters," reflecting a deep concern for "the

成 就

黄宗羲从"民本"立场抨击君主专制制度，主张立法为公，以"天下之法"取代"一家之法"，提出"天下为主，君为客"的民本思想。他的"新民本"思想超越了君主专制制度下传统儒家的"重民、爱民、为民请命"范式，具有近代法治观、民主观的萌芽。黄宗羲治学博通而精微，成就宏富，于经史百家、天文、历算、音律、释道、农工等均有深厚造诣。一生著述多达50余种、300余卷，其中较重要的有《南雷文定》《明儒学案》《宋元学案》《明夷待访录》等。

评 价

黄宗羲是明末清初杰出的启蒙思想家，也是成就卓著的哲学家、史学家、文学家。其思想体系重视"经世应务"，关心"万民忧乐"，超越了传统儒家框架，提出一系列具有启蒙性质的政治理论，包括对君主

welfare of all people." It transcended the traditional Confucian framework by proposing a series of politically enlightening theories, including criticism of autocratic monarchy and early explorations of democratic thought. Huang Zongxi's enlightening ideas exerted a significant influence on the Chinese reformist thoughts and democratic revolutions from the late Qing Dynasty to the modern times.

专制的批判和对民主思想的早期探索。黄宗羲对清末至近代的维新思潮和民主革命产生了重要影响。

Life Story

Shen Jiaben, courtesy name Zidun and ideal-expressing name Jiyi, hailed from Wuxing, was a native of Wuxing, Zhejiang (now Huzhou, Zhejiang) Province. His father Shen Bingying, who served as official of the Ministry of Justice and Prefect of Anshun in Guizhou, profoundly influenced his path in law. In the third year of the Tongzhi reign (1864), Shen Jiaben joined the Ministry of Justice as a probationary secretary. In 1865, he was admitted as a Juren (First-degree Scholar). During his tenure, he accumulated a wealth of case-handling experience and systematically compiled and studied ancient legal materials. During this time, he produced many legal and historical works, including *Miscellaneous Essays on Legal Codes* and *Studies on Criminal Law*. After becoming the Jinshi (Presented Scholar) in the ninth year of the Guangxu era (1883), Shen Jiaben served as the prefect of Tianjin and Baoding. In 1902, together with Wu Tingfang, he was tasked with presiding over the revision of laws and directing the affairs of the specialized bureau concerned with this matter. He presided over the formulation of a series of new laws, initiating China's legal modernization. He later became Chief Minister of the Council of Judicial Review and Minister in Charge of Legal Revisions, successively holding the positions of Right Vice Minister of the Law, Left Vice Minister of the Law, and Vice President of the Central Advisory Council. After the establishment of the Republic of China, he was nominated the Attorney General, but he declined the position and devoted himself to completing his final work, *Fragments of Laws of the Han Dynasty*. In June, 1913, Shen Jiaben passed away at his home in Beijing at the age of seventy-three.

生 平

沈家本，字子惇，别号寄簃，浙江吴兴（今浙江湖州）人。其父沈丙莹曾任刑部郎中、贵州安顺府知府对沈家本的法学兴趣和职业选择影响很大。清同治三年（1864年），沈家本入刑部任候补主事，1365年中举人，任职期间不仅积累了大量办案经验，也对古代法律资料进行了系统整理和研究，撰有众多经史考证和律学著作，如《律例杂说》《刑法杂考》等。光绪九年（1883年）中进士后升任刑部郎中，1893年至1900年先后出任天津、保定知府。1902年他与伍廷芳受命主持修律，总领修订法律馆事，主持制定一系列新法，开启了中国法律近代化进程。其间，先后任法部右侍郎、左侍郎、大理院正卿、修订法律大臣、资政院副总裁等职。民国成立后，沈家本曾被举荐出任司法总长，但辞未就职，潜心完成最后一部著述《汉律摭遗》。1913年6月，沈家本逝世于北京家中，终年七十三岁。

Contributions

The legal reforms of the late Qing dynasty (between 1902 and 1911) led by Shen Jiaben marked the beginning of China's legal modernization. After translating and studying the laws and jurisprudential works from more than ten Western countries, he revised outdated statutes and enacted new laws, abolishing centuries-old brutal punishments such as *Lingchi* (death by a thousand cuts) and decapitation. Under his leadership, the new laws were drafted, including *New Criminal Law of the Great Qing*, *Draft Civil Law of the Great Qing*, *Imperial Commercial Law of the Great Qing*, *Draft Code of the Criminal Procedure of the Great Qing*, *Draft Code of the Civil Procedure of the Great Qing*, and *Court Organization Law*. These reforms dismantled the traditional legal structure characterized by the fusion of various legal branches and the amalgamation of administrative and judicial powers. Shen was the first to propose the establishment of a modern adjudication system, the creation of the prosecutorial and lawyer system, the adoption of jury trials, as well as the modern legal principles such as freedom of contract, a legally prescribed punishment for a specified crime, commensuration of crime and punishment, and public trial. Furthermore, Shen Jiaben attached great importance to legal education. In 1906, he founded the Imperial Metropolitan Law College, a specialized law school directly under the Qing government, laying the foundation for modern legal education in China.

成 就

沈家本主导的清末修律（1902年—1911年）开启了中国法律近代化进程。他在翻译、研究西方十会个国家法律、法学著作的基础上，改造旧律、制定新法，废除了凌迟、枭首等酷刑，主持制定《大清新刑律》《大清民律草案》《钦定大清商律》《大清刑事民事诉讼法草案》《法院编制法》等新法，改变了传统法律制度中"诸法合体"、行政权与司法权混同等问题；首次提出构建近代审判制度，创设检察制度、律师制度、陪审制度，确立契约自由、罪刑法定、罪刑相适应、审判公开等现代法律原则。此外，沈家本还极为重视法学教育，1906年负责创办清廷直属法律专门学校——"京师法律学堂"，是近代中国法学教育体系化的开端。

Legacy   As the Minister of Legal Reforms and a renowned jurist in the late Qing Dynasty, Shen Jiaben made substantial contributions to the modernization of China's legal system, the jurisprudential development, and the cultivation of legal talents. During the legal reform movement in the late Qing Dynasty, he leveraged his profound knowledge of traditional Chinese law and comparative law studies to draw inspiration from ancient and modern sources, as well as Chinese and Western legal thoughts. He translated numerous foreign legal codes, extensively absorbed the strengths of Western legal systems, and oversaw the drafting of dozens of new laws. By introducing many modern legal principles and establishing modern corporate, commercial, lawyer, and jury systems, he played a crucial role in advancing the modernization of China's legal system. Therefore, the academia have revered him as the "matchmaker between Chinese and Western legal systems."

The former residence of Shen Jiaben at No.1 Jinjing Hutong, Xicheng District, Beijing, now serves as an educational site dedicated to promoting traditional Chinese legal culture.

评价

沈家本是清末修律大臣、晚清著名法学家，对中国法制近代化、法学繁荣和法律人才的培养，作出了很大贡献。在晚清变法修律浪潮中，他以深厚的传统法学功底和卓越的比较法学研究，参酌古今、融汇中西，大量翻译外国法律，广泛汲取西方法律所长，主持制定新法数十部，不仅引入了许多近代法律原则，还确立了近代公司、商事制度、律师、陪审制度等，对推动中国法制现代化进程起到了举足轻重的作用．被学届誉为"中西法制之冰人'。

沈家本故居位于北京市西城区金井胡同1号，目前已发展成为弘扬中华优秀传统法律文化的教育场所。

一纸书来只为墙
让他三尺又何妨
长城万里今犹在
不见当年秦始皇

六尺巷：
一诗化干戈

清朝康熙年间，文华殿大学士张英接到安徽桐城家书，族人与邻居因三尺宅基发生纠纷，争执不下。张英提笔回诗："一纸书来只为墙，让他三尺又何妨？长城万里今犹在，不见当年秦始皇。"张家见诗即退让三尺，邻居感其雅量亦让三尺，六尺巷道由此而生。这则载于《桐城县志略》的佳话展现了"以和为贵""天下无讼"的传统理念，也生动诠释了中华优秀传统法律文化中蕴含的解纷智慧。

The Six-foot Alley:
A Poem Turns Conflict into Harmony

During the reign of Emperor Kangxi of the Qing Dynasty, Zhang Ying, the Grand Secretary of Wenhua Hall, received a letter from his family in Tongcheng, Anhui. The letter was about a dispute between his relatives and their neighbors over a three-foot plot of land, with neither side willing to back down. Zhang Ying replied with a short poem, "A letter sent from afar over a wall—Why not concede a few feet after all? The Great Wall stretches thousands of miles, still standing tall, but where is Emperor Qin Shi Huang, who built it all?" Moved by his words, his family retreated three feet, and their neighbors, touched by this grace, did the same, thus creating a six-foot alleyway. Recorded in the *Annals of Tongcheng County*, this story manifests the traditional Chinese values of "prioritizing harmony" and "building a world without litigation." It vividly illustrates the dispute-resolution wisdom inherent in Chinese traditional legal culture.

【 参考文献 】

1. 司马迁:《史记》,中华书局 1959 年版。

2.《商君书》,中华书局 2009 年版。

3.《论语》,中华书局 2016 年版。

4.《管子》(全二册),中华书局 2019 年版。

5.《辞海》,上海辞书出版社 2009 年版。

6. 中国历史大辞典编纂委员会:《中国历史大辞典》,上海辞书出版社 2010 年版。

7. 中国大百科全书总编辑委员会《法学》编辑委员会:《中国大百科全书·法学卷》,中国大百科全书出版社 2020 年版。

8. 张晋藩:《中国法律思想史》,法律出版社 2004 年版。

9. 张晋藩:《中国法律史》,法律出版社 1995 年版。

10. 杨一凡:《中华法系研究·第十卷》,社会科学文献出版社 2018 年版。

11. [英] 李约瑟:《中国科学技术史(第六卷生物学与生物技术第六分册医学)》,科学出版社 2013 年版。

12. 沈小兰、蔡小雪:《修律大臣沈家本》,人民法院出版社 2012 年版。

图书在版编目（CIP）数据

法本：中华优秀传统法律文化图说：汉、英 / 人民法院出版社编 . -- 北京：人民法院出版社，2025.6. -- ISBN 978-7-5109-4416-1

Ⅰ . D920.5

中国国家版本馆CIP数据核字第2024Z80U10号

法本——中华优秀传统法律文化图说（中英文版）
人民法院出版社　编

总 策 划	余茂玉
编 写 人	张艳华
绘　　画	向　萌　焦亚娜
顾问单位	中国法律史学会
审　　定	最高人民法院国际合作局
中文审核	张　生　罗冠男　李　驰　李德嘉
责任编辑	余茂玉　尹立霞
执行编辑	孟祥男
英文翻译	潘　柔
英文审核	钱垂君　张　义
装帧设计	丁　鼎　王子莹
出版发行	人民法院出版社
地　　址	北京市东城区东交民巷 27 号（100745）
电　　话	010-67550637（责任编辑）
客服QQ	2092078039
网　　址	http://www.courtbook.com.cn
E－mail	courtpress@sohu.com
印　　刷	中煤（北京）印务有限公司
经　　销	新华书店
开　　本	787×1092 毫米　1/16
印　　张	13.75
插　　页	15 张
字　　数	68 千字
版　　次	2025 年 6 月第 1 版　2025 年 6 月第 1 次印刷
书　　号	ISBN 978-7-5109-4416-1
定　　价	98.00 元

版权所有　侵权必究